DLAB Practice & Skills Test Published on Amazon

© 2022

D1716011

Introduction:

This book will not teach you English. If you struggle with understanding and identifying verbs, objects, subjects, adjectives, adverbs, articles, the possessive forms of words, and understanding word syllable stress, then I highly recommend taking a quick detour before beginning and refreshing your knowledge on grammar and sentence structure. Having a strong understanding of grammar and sentence structure is one of the most important things you can do to prepare yourself for the exam in addition to these practice problems.

If all those terms where familiar, then let's begin. The aim of this book is to familiarize yourself with the format of the test by providing several hundred-practice problems.

IMPORTANT: The rules in these practice questions will NOT be the same rules you will see on your actual test, though they will be similar. Please keep that in mind on test day and read the instructions carefully! For that reason, I have broken each section into two groups (Group A and Group B) with different rule sets for each group. This will get you into the habit of seeing different types of rules for each section depending what is presented on the test.

The graded portion of the test consists of two parts, an audio and a visual portion.

Audio – 1 Stress Patterns

The first audio section requires to you identify stress patterns. Words can have entirely different meanings depending on where someone puts the stress on the syllable. For example, PRE-sent and pre-SENT, though spelled the same, are two very different words. During the test you will be presented with four options and asked to identify which of the option has a stress pattern different from the others.

Audio – Grammer Rules

The remaining audio sections will present you with a series of grammar rules that must be memorized and then applied to determine which option was correctly translated. You will only be shown the grammar rules at the beginning of each section.

Visual

During the visual portion of the test, you will be shown a series of images along with the corresponding translation. Your task is to correctly translate a different set of images based upon the already translated pictures.

Remember, this is a timed test, so please manage your time carefully. Unanswered questions are counted against you. You are also NOT allowed to go back and rehear an option once it has been read aloud. In this book, you are not given a time limit; your objective is to identify the patterns and answer as many questions correctly as possible. You will naturally pick up speed the more you practice.

For best results, I recommend having someone read the options aloud to you (preferably someone with a good grasp of the English language.) On test day: always be cognizant of your time and never leave a question blank.

Stress Patterns

Identify which of the four words has a stress pattern that is different than the others. You will not be shown the words on the actual test.

1.
   - A. Actor
   - B. Body
   - C. Mattress
   - D. Decay

2.
   - A. Christmas
   - B. Inspired
   - C. Involved
   - D. Compete

3.
   - A. Silly
   - B. Discuss
   - C. Tractor
   - D. Lizard

4.
   - A. Document
   - B. Optional
   - C. Obnoxious
   - D. Energy

5.
   - A. Employer
   - B. Contribute
   - C. Assignment
   - D. Scavenger

6.
- A. Enjoyment
- B. Nutritious
- C. Hydrogen
- D. Embracement

7.
- A. Baker
- B. Cosmetic
- C. Infections
- D. Appliance

8.
- A. Favorite
- B. Establish
- C. Excellence
- D. Glamorous

9.
- A. Poetry
- B. Cranberry
- C. Excellence
- D. Enjoyment

10.
- A. Graffiti
- B. Industry
- C. Trivial
- D. Lavender

11.
- A. Agreement
- B. Immature
- C. Advantage
- D. Recycle

12.
- A. Maniac
- B. Melody
- C. Migration
- D. Meteor

13.
- A. Volunteer
- B. Wonderful
- C. Horrify
- D. Membership

14.
- A. Humorous
- B. Messenger
- C. Difference
- D. Magnetic

15.
- A. Handicap
- B. Complexion
- C. Pharmacy
- D. Pedestal

16.
   A. Voluntary
   B. Technology
   C. Secretary
   D. Military

17.
   A. Violation
   B. Celebration
   C. Generation
   D. Aquarium

18.
   A. Professional
   B. Adversity
   C. Watermelon
   D. Belligerent

19.
   A. Obligation
   B. Population
   C. Photography
   D. Carolina

20.
   A. Degenerate
   B. Dictionary
   C. Ordinary
   D. Bodybuilding

21.

    A. Entertainment
    B. Antarctica
    C. Perspiration
    D. Education

22.

    A. Retirement
    B. Literature
    C. Television
    D. Agriculture

23.

    A. Obviously
    B. Alligator
    C. Necessary
    D. Integrity

24.

    A. Persecution
    B. Directory
    C. Relationship
    D. Canadian

25.

    A. Anonymous
    B. Community
    C. Termination
    D. Society

26.
- A. Mandatory
- B. Architecture
- C. Helicopter
- D. Delivery

27.
- A. Preposition
- B. Everlasting
- C. Democracy
- D. Relaxation

28.
- A. Alternative
- B. Information
- C. Eternity
- D. Anxiety

29.
- A. Independence
- B. Potassium
- C. Bureaucratic
- D. Disestablish

30.
- A. Circulatory
- B. Communicator
- C. Vocabulary
- D. Anticipated

31.
   A. Executioner
   B. Generosity
   C. Curiosity
   D. Administrator

32.
   A. Anniversary
   B. Sociology
   C. Biological
   D. Extraordinary

33.
   A. Organization
   B. Cafeteria
   C. Elimination
   D. Participation

34.
   A. Ramification
   B. Mathematician
   C. Understandable
   D. Intoxication

35.
   A. Parallelogram
   B. Perpendicular
   C. Intellectual
   D. Classification

36.
- A. Hospitality
- B. Degeneration
- C. Evaporation
- D. Louisiana

37.
- A. Radioactive
- B. Globalization
- C. Unidentified
- D. Procrastination

38.
- A. Diabolical
- B. Anticipation
- C. Infidelity
- D. Creativity

39.
- A. Astronomical
- B. Popularity
- C. Communication
- D. Personality

40.
- A. Execution
- B. Indecisive
- C. Undeniable
- D. Rationalize

41.
  A. Personification
  B. Deniability
  C. Accelerometer
  D. Involuntarily

42.
  A. Revolutionary
  B. Responsibility
  C. Identifiable
  D. Extraterrestrial

43.
  A. Encyclopedia
  B. Biodiversity
  C. Memorabilia
  D. Specifically

44.
  A. Identification
  B. Involuntarily
  C. Divisibility
  D. Biotechnology

45.
  A. Autobiography
  B. Biodegradable
  C. Adaptability
  D. Unimaginable

Nouns and Adjectives
Group A Rules

Identify which option has been correctly translated based upon the following grammar rules.

Rule 1: Articles are not included
Rule 2: Nouns and adjectives & verbs and adverbs have the same ending as the noun or vowel they modify
Rule 3: Adjectives and adverbs always comes after the noun or vowel

46. Black cat
    A. Blacko cato
    B. Cata blacko
    C. Cato blacko
    D. Blacka cat

47. The black cat
    A. Cato blacko
    B. The blacko cato
    C. The cato blacko
    D. Cata blacko

48. Cold beverage
    A. Coldy bevera
    B. Bevera colda
    C. Beverage coldy
    D. Colda beverage

49. Winter storm
    A. Wintera storma
    B. Storma wintere
    C. Stormy wintere
    D. Storma wintera
50. A tug boat
    A. Boata a tuga
    B. Boate tuga
    C. Boata tuga
    D. A boata tuga

51. A red fire truck
    A. Reda trucka fira
    B. Trucka fira reda
    C. Trucka a reda fira
    D. Trucka fire reda

52. Stop at the orange cone
    A. Stope cone orange
    B. Stope oranga cona
    C. Stopa a cona oranga
    D. Stopa oranga cona

53. The blue bus
    A. Blua busa
    B. The blua busa
    C. Busa blue
    D. Busa blua

54. Grab a red pen
    A. Grabo pene reda
    B. Grabo pene rede
    C. Graba reda pena
    D. Grabo a pene rede

55. The sly fox hid in the cave
    A. Slya foxa cave hida
    B. Foxa slaya hida in the cava
    C. Foxa slye cava hida
    D. Foxa slya hida cavo

56. Wash the dirty grey dog outside
    A. Washo dogo dirto greya outsido
    B. Washa dogo dirto greyo outsida
    C. Washa the dogo dirto greyo outsida
    D. Washo dirto dogo greyo outside

57. Red apple and yellow banana
    A. Apple rede and bannana yellowa
    B. Rede apple and bannana yellowa
    C. Appla rede and bannana yellowa
    D. Appla rede and bannana yellowe

58. Turn at the red sign
    A. Turn at the signa reda
    B. Turny signy redy
    C. Turny signee redy
    D. Turna reda signa

59. The tall kid drove a blue car
    A. Tallo kido drove cara blua
    B. Kkido tallo drove a cara blua
    C. Kido tallo drove cara blua
    D. Kido tallo drove blua cara

60. The fast car flipped on the turn
    A. Caro fasto flippe turna
    B. Fasta caro flippe turna
    C. The caro fasto flippe turne
    D. Fasto caro flippe turna

61. The spotted cat jumped
    A. Spote cate jumpo
    B. Cate spote jumpa
    C. Cate spota jumpa
    D. The cate spota jump

62. The tall women wore a red dress
    A. Womene telle wore dressa reda
    B. Womene telle wore a dressa reda
    C. Womene telle wore reda dressa
    D. Telle womene wore dresse reda

63. The small boy stood quickly
    A. The boye smalle stoode quickla
    B. Smalle boye stoode quickla
    C. Boye smalla stooda quickla
    D. Boye smalle stooda quickla

64. A green yard with a white picket fence
    A. A yarda greena a whita picketa fenca
    B. A yarde greene fenca pickete white
    C. Yarde greene fenca picketa whita
    D. Yarde greene a fenca picketa whita

65. Dan made a wood birdhouse
    A. Dana mado a birdhousa wooda
    B. Dana mada birdhousa wooda
    C. Dana mada birhousey woode
    D. Dana wooda birdhousa

Possessive
Group A Rules

Identify which option has been correctly translated based upon the following grammar rules.

Rule 4: The possessor always comes after the object being possessed
Rule 5: The possessor always ends with a "y"
Rule 6: The thing being possessed always ends in "s" or "t"

66. Tim's Car
    A. Timy caret
    B. Car Timy
    C. Caret Timy
    D. Caret Time

67. The Car of Tim
    A. Car Timy
    B. Caret Timy
    C. Care Timy
    D. Timy caret

68. The Captain's boat
    A. Boat captainey
    B. Boata captainey
    C. Boat captaine
    D. Captainey boat

69. Jay's mom
    A. Momet Jaye
    B. Jaye momet
    C. Momet Jai
    D. Momet Jay

70. Stakeholder's Coffee
    A. Coffees stakeholde
    B. Coffees stakeholdy
    C. Stakehold coffees
    D. Coffee stakeholder

71. A day's work
    A. Worket daye
    B. Day worket
    C. Day works
    D. Worket day

72. The team's coach
    A. Coachet teamy
    B. Coachet teame
    C. Coach teamy
    D. Teamy coachet

73. The dog's owner
    A. Dogey owner
    B. Ownes dogey
    C. Ownet doge
    D. Owne doge

74. Corner of 9th Street
    A. Cornes 9th streety
    B. 9th street corney
    C. 9th streety cornes
    D. 9th streety cornet

75. Hogan's hero

    A. Herot hogae
    A. Hogane herot
    B. Hoganey heros
    C. Herot hoganey

76. Ring of Thanos

    A. Rings thanose
    B. Ring thanosey
    C. Rings thanosey
    D. Rinset thanose

77. Fisherman's wharf

    A. Wharfs fishermant
    B. Wharfy fishermans
    C. Wharfy fishermant
    D. Wharfs fishermany

78. Ability of others

    A. Abilit otheray
    B. Ability others
    C. Ability otheray
    D. Otheray ability

79. America's Cup

    A. Cupt americay
    B. Cups america
    C. Cupt america
    D. Capt americae

80. Referee's Call

    A.   Referrey callt
    B.   Referres calls
    C.   Calls referrey
    D.   Callt referre

81. Book of David

    A.   Daniely Books
    B.   Daniely Bookt
    C.   Bookt Daniely
    D.   Book Daniely

82. Daniel's arm is broke

    A.   Daniely armt is broki
    B.   Army danielt is broki
    C.   Armt daniels is broki
    D.   Armt daniely is broki

83. The adventures of Tom and Bob

    A.   Adventures of tomy and bob
    B.   Adventurey tomt and bobt
    C.   Adventures tom and boby
    D.   Adventurs tomy and boby

84. The story of James

    A.   Stort jamey
    B.   Story james
    C.   Story of james
    D.   The storty of Jamey

85. David and Sally's dog

    A. Dogey davet and sallet
    B. Doget davidly and sally
    C. David and slley doget
    D. Doget david and sally

86. Lauren's presentation went well

    A. Presentationy laurens wenta welli
    B. Presentations laurnet welli wenta
    C. Presentationy wenta welli Laurenat
    D. Presentat laureny wenta welli

87. Steve's dog ran away

    A. Stevet dogy rane awayo
    B. Dogt Stevey rane awayo
    C. Stevey dogt rane awayo
    D. Dogy Stevet rane awayo

Subjects, Verbs, Objects
Group A Rules

Identify which option has been correctly translated based upon the following grammar rules.

Rule 7: The subject has "ee" in the middle
Rule 8: The object ends with an "i"
Rule 9: Verbs end with a "u" or "a"

88. Jason ran to the store

    A. Jason ranu stori
    B. Jason ranu to the stori
    C. Jaseen ranu stori
    D. Jaseen ran stori

89. The teacher taught the class

    A. The teacher taughtu classi
    B. Teeacher taughta classi
    C. Teacher taughtu classi
    D. Teeacher taughta the classy

90. The ball broke the window

    A. Beel broke the windowi
    B. Baell broka windowi
    C. Baall broka windowi
    D. Beell broku windowi

91. Aaron climbed the rope

    A. Aareen climbi ropu
    B. Aareen climbi ropa
    C. Aaran climbu ropi
    D. Aareen climbu ropi

92. Karen kicked the ball

    A. Kareen kicka ball
    B. Kareen kicku balli
    C. Karen kicka balle
    D. Kareen kicku balle

93. Derek played the clarinet

    A. Derek playa the clarineti
    B. Deerek played clarineti
    C. Dereek playa clarineti
    D. Deerek play clarineti

94. Bob mowed the yard for Frank

    A. Boeeb mowa yardi for Franki
    B. Boeb mowu the yardi for Franki
    C. Boeeb mowu yarda franka
    D. Boeeb mowa the yardu for Franku

95. Tom moved the table for Rachel

    A. Toem mova tabli for Racheli
    B. Toeem mova tabli for Racheli
    C. Toeem movi the tabli for Racheli
    D. Toem mova the table for Racheli

96. The batter swung at the ball

    A. Batter swunga balli
    B. Bateeter swungi balla
    C. Bateeter wungi ballu
    D. Bateeter swunga balli

97. Steve picked apples and oranges

    A. Steeve picka appli and orangi
    B. Steeve picki appla and oranga
    C. Steeve picka appli and oranges
    D. Steve picka appli and orange

98. Mary sipped coffee and ate donuts

    A. Meery sipi coffa ati donuta
    B. Meery sipped coffe ata donuti
    C. Meery sipa coffi ata donuti
    D. Meery sipa coffa and ata donuti

99. Jess swept and mopped the floor

    A. Jes swepa and mopa floori
    B. Jess swepa mopi floori
    C. Jees swepa mopy the floori
    D. Jees swepu mopa floori

100. Tim and Allen ate oranges

    A. Tieem and Alleen ati oranga
    B. Tieem and Allen ata orangi
    C. Tieem Alleen atu orangi
    D. Tim Alleen ata orange

101. He wrote a letter

    A. Hee wrota letteri
    B. Hee wrote letteri
    C. He wrota letteri
    D. Hee wrotu lettery

102. He and I watched the show

    A. Hee and lee watchu showi
    B. He and lee watchu showi
    C. Hee and lee watchi showa
    D. Hee and I watcha showi

103. Paula stopped at the store

    A. Peela stopi stora
    B. Peela stopa a stori
    C. Paulea stopa stori
    D. Peela stopu a story

104. Craig went to the mall

    A. Crag wentu tu malle
    B. Craeeg wenti to the malli
    C. Craeeg wentu tu malla
    D. Craeeg wenta ta malli

105. Grab a notebook and pen

    A. Grabu notebooki and peni
    B. Greeb notebooki and peni
    C. Greeb notebooki and pene
    D. Graba notebook and peni

106. The baby cried loudly

    A. Beebe criedu loudly
    B. Babi criedu loudli
    C. Beebe criedi loudu
    D. The beebe cried loudly

107. He answered the question slowly

    A. Hee answere the questioni slewly
    B. Hee answera questoni slewly
    C. Hea answeru questioni slewla
    D. Hee answeru questionu slewli

108. The dog looked at Alex and growled

    A. Deeg looki at aleex and growli
    B. Deeg looka at aleex and growli
    C. Deeg looka at alexi and growla
    D. Deeg look alexi and growli

109. Scott cut the grass while Kyle trimmed the bushes

    A. Sceet cutu the grassi while Kyle trimma bushi
    B. Sceet cutu grassa while Kyle trimma bushi
    C. Sceet cutu grassi while Kyle etrimmi busha
    D. Sceet cutu grassi whila Keele trimu bushi

Comprehensive
Group A Rules

Identify which option has been correctly translated based upon the following grammar rules.

Rule 1: Articles are not included
Rule 2: Nouns and adjectives & verbs and adverbs have the same ending as the noun or vowel they modify
Rule 3: Adjectives and adverbs always comes after the noun or vowel
Rule 4: The possessor always comes after the object being possessed
Rule 5: The possessor always ends with a "y"
Rule 6: The thing being possessed always ends in "s" or "t"
Rule 7: The subject has "ee" in the middle
Rule 8: The object ends with an "i"
Rule 9: Verbs end with a "u" or "a"

110. Henry walked the dog

   A. Henry walk the dogi
   B. Henry walk dogi
   C. Heenry walka dogi
   D. Heenry walke dogi

111. Henry walked the small dog

   A. Heenry walka the doge smalle
   B. Heenry walka dogi smalli
   C. Heenry walka dogi smalla
   D. Heenry walka smalli dogi

112. The blue paper fell to the floor

    A. Blue papeera fella floori
    B. Papeere bluee fella floori
    C. Papeera blue fella floori
    D. Papeere bluee fella flooree

113. The quick cat stared at the sad man

    A. Ceeto quicko stara mani sadi
    B. Ceeto quicko stara sadi mani
    C. Quicko ceeto stara the mani sadi
    D. Ceeto quicko stari mana sada

114. Roger's blue car

    A. Cart blut rogey
    B. Cari bluee Rogey
    C. Blui cari Rogey
    D. Reeger cart blut

115. Tom ran quickly

    A. Toeem quicki rani
    B. Toeem rana quicka
    C. Toeem rana quicki
    D. Toeem quicki rana

116. The orange cat crossed the street

    A. Ceeto orangi crossa the streeti
    B. Orango ceeto crossa streeti
    C. Ceeta orange crossa streeti
    D. Ceeto orango crossa street

117. The round blue ball

    A. Roundo ballo bluo
    B. Roundi bluo ballo
    C. Ballo roundo bluo
    D. Ballo roundo blue

118. Wes talked about sports

    A. Wees talkao about sporti
    B. Wees talka abouti sporte
    C. Wees talka aboute sporti
    D. Wes talka aboute sporti

119. Phil shouts at the bad dog

    A. Pheel shouta ato dogi badi
    B. Phel shouta ato dogi bade
    C. Phel shouta ato the bade dogi
    D. Pheel shouta ato badi dogi

120. Rachel's lanyard

    A. Reechel lanyart
    B. Rachey lanyart
    C. Lanyart Reechey
    D. Lanyard Rachey

121. The Lion's big den

    A. Denes biges liony
    B. Denet biges liony
    C. Liony biges denes
    D. Leen denets biges

122. The little girl picked chocolate sauce

    A. Geerl little picku chocolata sauca
    B. Geerl little picka chocolate sauci
    C. Littel geerl picku sauci chocolate
    D. Geerl littel picku sauci chocolati

123. Nick lost the old t-shirt

    A. Neeck losta t-shirti oli
    B. Neck losta t-shirti oldi
    C. Neeck losta the t-shirti oli
    D. Neeck losta olda t-shirti

124. The office of Logan

    A. Officet Logany
    B. Logany officet
    C. The officet Logany
    D. Leegan office

125. Matt gave Erica a gift

    A. Meett gava Erica gifti
    B. Meett gava Erici a gifti
    C. Meett gava Ereeca gifti
    D. Meett gava Erici gifti

126. The tall man's hat

    A. Many hat tally
    B. Heta mani talla
    C. Hat many tally
    D. Tally many hati

127. Laura went to the grocery store

    A. Leero wenta groceri stori
    B. Leero wenta stori groceri
    C. Leero wenta grocero stori
    D. Leero wenta stori grocero

128. Tina has short curly brown hair

    A. Teena ha hai brown curlo shorto
    B. Teena ha hai browni curli shorti
    C. Teena ha hai curlo browni shorti
    D. Tena ha hai browni curli shorti

129. The white pickup truck ran the red light

    A. Treek pickupk whitek ranu the lighti redi
    B. Treek pickup white ranu lighti redi
    C. Treek pickupk whitek ranu lighti redi
    D. Pickup whitep treep rana lighti redi

Nouns and Adjectives
Group B Rules

Identify which option has been correctly translated based upon the following grammar rules.

Rule 1B: Articles are not included
Rule 2B: Nouns and adjectives & verbs and adverbs have the same ending as the noun or vowel they modify
Rule 3B: Adjectives and adverbs always comes after the noun or verb

130. The cunning fox chased the rabbit

    A. Foxa cunna chaso rabbito
    B. Foxey cunne rabbito chaso
    C. Foxa cunna chaso the rabbito
    D. The foxa cunna chaso rabbito

131. The skillful driver avoided the collision

    A. Skillfula drivera avoido the collisiona
    B. Drivera skillfula avoido collisiona
    C. The skillfula drivera avoida the collisiona
    D. Drivera skillfule avoida collisiona

132. Studious students earn good grades

    A. Studenta studia earna gooda grada
    B. Studenta studia earna grade gooda
    C. Studenta studia earna grada gooda
    D. Studia studenta earna grada gooda

133. The couple had a lovely time

    A. Coupla lovela timea
    B. Coupla a timea lovela
    C. The coupla timea lovela
    D. Coupla timea lovela

134. The interviewer's blunt question went unanswered

    A. The inverviewere questione blunte went unanswered
    B. Interviewerea questiona blunte went unanswered
    C. Interviewerea questiona blunta went unanswered
    D. Interviewerea blunta questiona went unanswered

135. They hired him for his strong performance

    A. They hireae for performa stronga
    B. Hireae for stronga performa
    C. They hireae for a performa stronge
    D. They hireae for performe stronga

136. The crowd cheered loudly

    A. The crowde cheere loudle
    B. Crowde cheere loudle
    C. Crowde loudle cheere
    D. Crowde loudle cheera

137. Tim threw the rotten egg

    A. Tim threwa the eggo rotteno
    B. Tim threwa rotteno eggo
    C. Tim threw rottene egga
    D. Tim threwa eggo rotteno

138. The small boy ran past the iron gate

    A. Boya smalla ran pasta irone gata
    B. Boya smalla ran pasta gate irone
    C. Smalla Boya ran pasta gate irone
    D. Boya small ran pasta the gata irona

139. The large fan blew hot air

    A. The fana larga blew aire hotte
    B. Fana larga blew hotte aire
    C. Larga fana blew aire hotte
    D. Fana larga blew aire hotte

140. Steve mopped the dirty floor

    A. Steve moppe the floore dirte
    B. Steve moppe floore dirte
    C. Moppe steve floore dirta
    D. Steve moppe dirta floora

141. The empty house was quiet

    A. The house empte was quieto
    B. House empta was quieta
    C. House empte was quieta
    D. Empte house was quiete

142. The catcher missed the wild pitch

    A. Catchere misse the pitche wilda
    B. Catchere misse the pitcha wilda
    C. Catchere missa wilda pitcha
    D. Catchere misse pitcha wilda

143. The shiny bell was rung

    A. The bella shina was runga
    B. Shine belle was runga
    C. Shina belle was runga
    D. Bella shina was runga

144. The shy girl wore a blue bonnet

    A. Girla shya wore bonneta bluea
    B. Shya girla wore bonneta bluea
    C. Girla shya wore a bonneta bluea
    D. Girla shya wore bluea bonneta

145. The smooth ball flew into the air

    A. Smoothe balle flew inte aire
    B. Balle smoothe flew inte aire
    C. Balle smootha flew inte aire
    D. The balle smoothe flew inte airea

146. The big green ball

    A. Biggie balla green
    B. Ballel greenel bigel
    C. Bigge ballel greenel
    D. The ballel greenel bigel

147. Stopped slowly

    A. Slowlo stopo
    B. Stopo slowle
    C. Stopo slowlo
    D. Slowle stopo

148. Slowly stopped

    A. Stopo slowlo
    B. Slowle stopo
    C. Slowlo stopo
    D. Stopo slowle

149. A yellow bird

    A. Birdow yellow
    B. Yellow birdow
    C. A birdow yellow
    D. Birdo yellow

Possessive
Group B Rules

Identify which option has been correctly translated based upon the following grammar rules.

Rule 4B: The possessor comes after the item being possessed
Rule 5B: The possessor ends with a "i"
Rule 6B: The object being possessed always ends "a" or "u"

150. The book of David

    A. Booka David
    B. Davidi booka
    C. Booku davidi
    D. Booky davidi

151. The newsman's desk

    A. Desky newsmans
    B. Desku newsmani
    C. Newant desky
    D. Newmani deska

152. The cardholder's right

    A. Rights cardholdery
    B. Cardholderi righu
    C. Rightt cardholdery
    D. Righta cardholderi

153. A gentleman's game

  A. Game gentlemani
  B. Gami gentlemani
  C. Gama gentlemani
  D. Gamu gentlemany

154. Attorney's fee

  A. Fea attornei
  B. Fea attorney
  C. Fees attorney
  D. Fei attorney

155. Throw Stone's frisbee away

  A. Throws frisbea stoney away
  B. Throwa frisbee stoni awaya
  C. Throwa frisbea stoni away
  D. Throwa stoni frisbea away

156. Hansel and Gretel's Story

  A. Story Hansela and Gretela
  B. Stora Hanseli and Greteli
  C. Hansel and stora greteli
  D. Hansel and stort Gretely

157. Children's toys

  A. Tou childreni
  B. Toy childrens
  C. Toa childrens
  D. Toy children

158. Owl's eye

    A. Owly eyes
    B. Eye owli
    C. Eyu owli
    D. Owli eyu

159. Eye of the Owl

    A. Owli eyu
    B. Eyu owli
    C. Owly eyes
    D. Eye owli

160. Media's influence

    A. Influenca media
    B. Media influenci
    C. Influenca medi
    D. Influency medi

161. Recipient's name

    A. Name receipi
    B. Receipi namu
    C. Nama receipi
    D. Nama receipy

162. Board of trustees

    A. Borda trustee
    B. Boardu trusti
    C. Trusta boardi
    D. Trusti borda

163. Mom and Dad's car

    A. Caru momi and dadi
    B. Cary momy and dadi
    C. Caru momy and dady
    D. Momi and caru dadi

164. Dogs' treats

    A. Treatu dogy
    B. Treat dogi
    C. Doga treati
    D. Treta dogi

165. Hal's house

    A. Hali housa
    B. Housa halu
    C. Housa hali
    D. Hali house

166. Hall of heros

    A. Halli hera
    B. Halla heri
    C. Heri halla
    D. Heru halla

167. The Sheriff's officers

    A. Officeri sheriffa
    B. Sherifi officera
    C. Sheriffa officeri
    D. Officeru sherifi

168. The recruit's record

    A. Recordi recruita
    B. Recordu recruiti
    C. Recorde recruiti
    D. Recruiti record

169. The clown's joke

    A. Joka clownee
    B. Jokee clowna
    C. Clowni joka
    D. Joka clowni

170. Mom's pie

    A. Piu momi
    B. Momi pia
    C. Momu pia
    D. Pie momi

171. Dan and Tom's adventures

    A. Adventuri Dan y Tomi
    B. Dane y Tomi adventura
    C. Adventura Dani y Tomi
    D. Dani adventura tomi

Subjects, Verbs, Objects
Group B Rules

Identify which option has been correctly translated based upon the following grammar rules.

Rule 7: The subject has an "aa" or "ee" in the middle
Rule 8: The object ends in "e"
Rule 9: Verbs begin with "ya" and never end with a "s"

172. Sarah ordered a drink

    A. Sarah yarded drink
    B. Saarah yardered drinke
    C. Saarah yardered a drinka
    D. Saarah yardereds drinke

173. Bob fell

    A. Beeb yafell
    B. Bob yafell
    C. Yafell Bob
    D. Beeb yafells

174. Keith worked at the market

    A. Keith yaworked at the markete
    B. Yaworks keeith markete
    C. Keeith yaworked market
    D. Keeith yaworked markete

175. Nelson bought a ticket

    A. Neelson yabought tickete
    B. Neelson yabought ticket
    C. Nelson yabought a tickete
    D. Neelson yaboughts tickete

176. The car crashed into the wall

    A. Caer yacrashed into the walle
    B. Caeer yacrashed into walle
    C. Caeer yacrasheds into walle
    D. The caeer yacrashed into the wall

177. The rocket launched into space

    A. rockeet yalauncheds into space
    B. Rockeet yalaunched into spaca
    C. Rocket yalaunched into space
    D. Rockeet yalaunched into space

178. The team evaluated proposals

    A. Team yaevaluat proposals
    B. Teeam yaevaluat proposala
    C. Teeam yaevaluat proposale
    D. Teeam yaevaluats proposal

179. I drove my vehicle while she rode the bus

    A. Iee yadrove mi vehicle while shee yarode the bus
    B. Iee yadrove mi vehicla while shee yarode buse
    C. Iee yadrove mi vehicule while shee rode buse
    D. Iee yadrove mi vehicle while shee yarode buse

180. Steve and Simon rode horses

    A. Steeve and Simeen yarode horse
    B. Steve and Simeen yarode horsts
    C. Steve and Simeen yarodes horse
    D. Steve and Simeen yarode horse

181. He typed rapidly on the keyboard

    A. Hee yatyped rapida on keyboard
    B. Hea yatyped rapida on keyboardo
    C. Hee yatyped rapido on keyboarde
    D. Hee typed rapido on the keyboarde

182. Run to the store

    A. Yarun toe store
    B. Yarun toe stora
    C. Yaruns toe store
    D. Raan toe store

183. John played chess on his boat

    A. Jeehn yaplayed chesse on his boat
    B. Jeehn yaplayed chesse on his boate
    C. Jeehn yaplayed chess on his boate
    D. John yaplayed chesse on hisa boate

184. Jerry studied calculus and physics

    A. Jeerry yastudied calculus and physice
    B. Jerry yastudies calculus and physice
    C. Jeerry yastudied calcule and physice
    D. Jeerry yastudied calcule and physics

185. Laura hopped and skipped down the street

    A. Leera yahopped and yaskipped down streete
    B. Leera yahopped and yaskipped downa the street
    C. Leera yahopped and yaskipps downa street
    D. Leera yahopped and skipped downa street

186. Tory and David ate chips and salsa

    A. Teery and Deevid yate chipe and salse
    B. Teery and Deevid yate chips and salse
    C. Teery and Deevid yates chips and salse
    D. Teery and David yate chipe and salse

187. The dog chased the ball

    A. Dog yachased balle
    B. Daag yachas balle
    C. Daag yachased ball
    D. Daag yachased balle

188. The dog chased and barked at the boy

    A. Daag yachased and yabarked at the boy
    B. Daag yachased and barka ata boye
    C. Daag yachasas and yabarkas at boye
    D. Daag yachased and yabarked at boye

189. Riley talks to Ann

    A. Raaly yatalk to Anne
    B. Riley yatalks to Anne
    C. Raaly yatlaks to anne
    D. Raaly yatalk to Anna

190. Riley talked to Ann about sports

    A. Riley yatalks to ann about a sporte
    B. Raaly yatalk to anne about sporte
    C. Raaly yatalks to anne about a sporte
    D. Raaly yatalk to anna about sports

191. Tory washed and rinsed the dished

    A. Taary washed and yarinsed dishe
    B. Taary yawashed and yarinsed dishe
    C. Taary yawashed and yarinsed dishes
    D. Taary yawashed and yarins the dishe

192. Craig ran down the stairs and tripped on a step

    A. Craaig yaran down staire y yatripped on stepe
    B. Craaig yaran down stairs y yatripped on stepe
    C. Craaig yaran down stairs yatripps on stepe
    D. Craaig yaran down staire y tripped on a stepe

193. The car slid across the highway

    A. Car yaslid across highwe
    B. Caar slid across the highwe
    C. Caar yaslid across highwe
    D. Caar yaslid across highway

Comprehensive
Group B Rules

Identify which option has been correctly translated based upon the following grammar rules.

Rule 1B: Articles are not included
Rule 2B: Nouns and adjectives, & verbs and adverbs have the same ending as the noun or vowel they modify
Rule 3B: Adjectives and adverbs always comes after the noun or verb
Rule 4B: The possessor comes after the item being possessed
Rule 5B: The possessor end in "i"
Rule 6B: The object being possessed always ends "a" or "u"
Rule 7B: The subject has an "aa" or "ee" in the middle
Rule 8B: The object ends in "e"
Rule 9B: Verbs begin with "ya" and never end with a "s"

194. Laura sent the email
    A. Laura yasent email
    B. Laaura yasent the emaile
    C. Laaura yasent email
    D. Laaura yasent emaile

195. Laura sent Gabe a letter

    A. Laaura yasent Gabe lettore
    B. Laaura yasent Gaba lettera
    C. Laaura yasent Gabe a lettere
    D. Laaura yasents Gabe lettore

196. Carter's letter arrived

    A. Laatera Caarteri yarrived
    B. Laateri Caartera yarrived
    C. Leetero Caartera yarrived
    D. Caarter leetera yarrived

197. Stacy kicks the winning goal

    A. Staacey yakick wine goale
    B. Staacey yakick goale wine
    C. Staacey yakicks wine goale
    D. Staacey yakicks goale wine

198. Lin laughed at the awkward joke

    A. Laan yalaugh ato the joke akwarde
    B. Laan yalaugh ato akwardo joke
    C. Laan yalaugh ato joke akwarde
    D. Lean yalaugh ato joke akwarde

199. The little fish quickly swam

    A. Faash little yawam quickim
    B. Faash litteh yaswam quick
    C. Faash littlo quick yaswam
    D. Faash littleh yaswam quickim

200. The group's leader was Tim

    A. Groupi leedi yas Time
    B. Laada graapi yas Time
    C. Laada grapa ya Time
    D. Laada graapi ya Time

201. The brown fox jumped the fence

    A. Brown faaxo yajump fence
    B. Faaxo braawno yajump fence
    C. Faaxe brawwno yajump fence
    D. Faaxo brawwno yajump the fenca

202. Jane and Jack studied for the test

    A. Jaane y Jaack yastudy for teste
    B. Jaane y Jack yastudy for teste
    C. Jaane y Jaack yastudy for the teste
    D. Jane y Jaack yastudy for teste

203. Jay passed the history test

    A. Jaay yapassed historo teste
    B. Jaay yapassed teste histore
    C. Jaay yapassed teste historo
    D. Jay yapassed teste histore

204. Tory runs and swims

    A. Taary yaruns yaswims
    B. Taary yaruns y yaswim
    C. Taary yarune y yaswimo
    D. Tary yarune y yaswimo

205. Sean quickly moved the box

    A. Seaan quickle yamove boxe
    B. Sean yamoves quickle boxe
    C. Seaan yamove quickle boxe
    D. Seaan yamove quickle the box

206. Sean moved the box quickly

    A. Seaan yamove boxe quicke
    B. Sean yamove quickle boxe
    C. Seaan yamove boxe quickla
    D. Seaan yamoves quicka boxe

207. The ball landed in Tony's yard

    A. Baal yaland ino yarda Toni
    B. Baal land ino yarda Tone
    C. Baal yaland ino Toni yarde
    D. Baal yaland ino yarde Tony

208. Diane threw a ball

    A. Diane yathrews balle
    B. Diaane yathrew a balle
    C. Diane yathrew balle
    D. Diaane yathrew balle

209. Little Timmy picked the Christmas tree

    A. Littey Tammy yapick tree Christme
    B. Taamy littey yapick tree Christme
    C. Taamy litte yapick tree Christme
    D. Taamy lettey yapick the tree Christme

210. The wolf loudly howled

    A. Waalf loudel yahowl
    B. Waalf yahowl loudal
    C. Waalf loude yahowl
    D. The waalf loudel yahowl

211. Derek bought apples and oranges

    A. Daarek yabought applas y orange
    B. Daarek yabought appla y orange
    C. Daarek yaboughts apple y orange
    D. Daarek yabought apple y orange

212. The little baby cried

    A. Baabe little yacried
    B. Baaby little yacried
    C. The baabe little yacried
    D. Little baabe yacried

213. The dentist's office

    A. The offica dentisti
    B. Dentisti offica
    C. Offica dentisti
    D. Daantist officu

Visual

Use the four translated images and the picture set to translate the corresponding questions. There are 3 questions for each set.

lelanding   cation   egnardo   sealy

214.

    A. Seagon
    B. Martion
    C. Irnardo
    D. Egedia

215.

    A. Letion
    B. Plardo
    C. Seon
    D. Catly

216.

    A. Lenardo
    B. Seardo
    C. Ration
    D. Lely

cation

doric

lever

loraket

217.

    A. Ketlic
    B. Dorayme
    C. Tioner
    D. Catlic

218.

    A. Rowly
    B. Levtion
    C. Vestion
    D. Rayroric

219.

    A. Virtuo
    B. Kroket
    C. Dover
    D. Silec

levant

cupity

marance

anaress

220.

- A. Ocial
- B. Maress
- C. Leroy
- D. Cuance

221.

- A. Curess
- B. Lerance
- C. Anacu
- D. Redant

222.

- A. Vanmar
- B. Anacu
- C. Marvance
- D. Marity

entlow

cohip

etsrite

rorect

223.

- A. Colow
- B. Etrect
- C. Rohip
- D. Hiplow

224.

- A. Entrite
- B. Corite
- C. Etrect
- D. Etlow

225.

- A. Entrite
- B. Corite
- C. Ethip
- D. Entrect

belcrow

revo

letina

bantish

226.

    A. Bancrow
    B. Belvo
    C. Retish
    D. Reina

227.

    A. Bantina
    B. Beltish
    C. Votina
    D. Tinavo

228.

    A. Beltish
    B. Bantina
    C. Tishvo
    D. Lecrow

sovil   letina   nanite   revo

229.

- A. Tian
- B. Sovo
- C. Letite
- D. Levil

230.

- A. Nanina
- B. Sovite
- C. Navo
- D. Revo

231.

- A. Revolin
- B. Rovil
- C. Torite
- D. Lenite

besles

cining

dackage

cubern

232.
    A. Baring
    B. Barlow
    C. Besrel
    D. Bustern

233. —
    A. Cinol
    B. Besage
    C. Dolern
    D. Dacking

234.
    A. Cubes
    B. Cublet
    C. Cubing
    D. Cubage

prodox   clesk   spongent   elvand

235.
    A. Dadox
    B. Pregent
    C. Pokem
    D. Rongent

236.
    A. Elegent
    B. Cleand
    C. Sponox
    D. Clegent

237.
    A. Countesk
    B. Rumvand
    C. Engin
    D. Vangent

nanite

entum

localmist

rorect

238.
    A. Nanect
    B. Yotem
    C. Nantum
    D. Hilbite

239.
    A. Entmist
    B. Rocundum
    C. Valite
    D. Relum

240.
    A. Telmo
    B. Kelven
    C. Nanect
    D. Morside

karado   stradum   kunia   eisder

241.

- A. Karia
- B. Eisdo
- C. Kundo
- D. Karadum

242.

- A. Kunsto
- B. Straly
- C. Misder
- D. Nado

243.

- A. Strawber
- B. Karader
- C. Eising
- D. Strader

sapor

browben

dudant

choly

244.

    A. Sadant
    B. Chopor
    C. Porben
    D. Saben

245.

    A. Chodant
    B. Dupor
    C. Shodant
    D. Rowben

246.

    A. Dudint
    B. Chodar
    C. Porlic
    D. Benpha

entlow

loraket

krone

baroll

247.

    A. Lelow
    B. Entoll
    C. Lowon
    D. Loralow

248.

    A. Krolow
    B. Lorone
    C. Kroll
    D. Entol

249.

    A. Entol
    B. Barly
    C. Serol
    D. Valen

anagate

credi

desloit

terrix

250.

   A. Anadi
   B. Analoit
   C. Terdi
   D. Desgate

251.

   A. Desix
   B. Analoit
   C. Foloit
   D. Creloit

252.

   A. Creter
   B. Dester
   C. Spedrix
   D. Creix

socumdia cassil coropo welanbe

253.

    A. Veredum
    B. Recumdo
    C. Merceko
    D. Hilbosco

254.

    A. Capo
    B. Robe
    C. Sossbe
    D. Cupo

255.

    A. Ketdobum
    B. Subeak
    C. Febsodum
    D. Gelanem

coropo

nanite

thelor

entlow

256.

- A. Color
- B. Coronite
- C. Nalor
- D. Entite

257.

- A. Nalor
- B. Nalow
- C. Thelow
- D. Lorna

258.

- A. Roitlow
- B. Lona
- C. Entite
- D. Polow

trollegic chehalin dimozen emvidon

259.

    A. Remozen
    B. Tremoza
    C. Shilegic
    D. Dividic

260.

    A. Ditulin
    B. Comrollzen
    C. Chevidic
    D. Dillegin

261.

    A. Emlegdon
    B. Meherin
    C. Enviden
    D. Copodon

pretue   mivilen   dudant   anaress

262.

- A. Previltue
- B. Anertue
- C. Bometue
- D. Predolen

263.

- A. Sivilen
- B. Midu
- C. Renarvil
- D. Helenmi

264.

- A. Duarlen
- B. Anviless
- C. Dunarmist
- D. Temeress

localmist

estrite

thelor

cation

265.

    A. Lolon
    B. Shecaler
    C. Tomista
    D. Mucalon

266.

    A. Entrite
    B. Estlor
    C. Lorite
    D. Riteguin

267.

    A. Thetist
    B. Catlorite
    C. Belorca
    D. Therion

chical   rorect   lelanding   camdo

268.

    A. Dorect
    B. Secal
    C. Trichi
    D. Pordo

269.

    A. Leromen
    B. Rolandal
    C. Robendo
    D. Selanect

270.

    A. Camvanect
    B. Moaming
    C. Calando
    D. Camring

rerany lelanding lomechen anaress

271.

    A. Posupess
    B. Atmenra
    C. Relechen
    D. Inrado

272.

    A. Lecorany
    B. Somecing
    C. Lolandess
    D. Camchen

273.

    A. Anachen
    B. Recomo
    C. Sonarly
    D. Anaring

crical

burel

broben

lusca

274.

- A. Penca
- B. Wato
- C. Stucal
- D. Perlus

275.

- A. Raben
- B. Burca
- C. Sodrel
- D. Brorel

276.

- A. Bencrilow
- B. Brovemal
- C. Calval
- D. Rescal

spomerken

clesk

trollegic

scilatay

277.

    A. Tromeray
    B. Clekenic
    C. Antroday
    D. Picelic

278.

    A. Pharmeray
    B. Piben
    C. Spolegic
    D. Schspo

279.

    A. Pasesk
    B. Scimeray
    C. Scilegesk
    D. Clelatca

.

bulenest

climbo

terix

rorect

280.

- A. Awtrix
- B. Spidet
- C. Terknest
- D. Bulrix

281.

- A. Clistager
- B. Ronest
- C. Rolabo
- D. Clirix

282.

- A. Bulbo
- B. Confest
- C. Solema
- D. Terimbul

stawelen

bantish

ornerag

astistment

283.

    A. Denerment
    B. Larbanag
    C. Orneren
    D. Clitag

284.

    A. Qulolen
    B. Banerwel
    C. Statist
    D. Astelow

285.

    A. Astnerish
    B. Astweban
    C. Banartment
    D. Baneragment

belcumin

frolitber

senressive

novitcal

286.

- A. Shincucal
- B. Frofircal
- C. Nocusive
- D. Senlitber

287.

- A. Senvitrol
- B. Novlitmin
- C. Frotrossive
- D. Monive

288.

- A. Belitcal
- B. Debelor
- C. Savrebel
- D. Anwomin

duvestard

remusment

intcrador

senressive

289.

- A. Pripather
- B. Sencratard
- C. Covestive
- D. Ducrament

290.

- A. Rusidard
- B. Verflument
- C. Elpaly
- D. Precowdor

291.

- A. Intvessive
- B. Demusetol
- C. Recodor
- D. Opmusard

manrila

chehalin

exrowen

wastoner

292.

    A. Firawen
    B. Mananer
    C. Forhan
    D. Chexisly

293.

    A. Cherower
    B. Chetonly
    C. Innertone
    D. Wasrolat

294.

    A. Stuloyer
    B. Garowlin
    C. Nawtonor
    D. Swirila

cresslo

peticent

cepabed

ofatly

295.

    A. Frissly
    B. Cressent
    C. Creably
    D. Baticent

296.

    A. Peloed
    B. Atlo
    C. Peatdon
    D. Tecremal

297.

    A. Cepan
    B. Oprement
    C. Verated
    D. Forlobed

frolitber

crenolo

scilatay

anaress

298.

    A. Stober
    B. Chimotay
    C. Creamtay
    D. Scilober

299.

    A. Crebanar
    B. Sinatay
    C. Frohelo
    D. Expaber

300.

    A. Anmortay
    B. Crelitow
    C. Crehelress
    D. Ressmacre

ANSWERS

1. **D**
   A. AC-tor
   B. BOD-y
   C. MAT-tress
   D. de-CAY

2. **A**
   A. CHRIST-mas
   B. in-SPIRED
   C. in-VOLVED
   D. com-PETE

3. **B**
   A. SILL-y
   B. di-SCUSS
   C. TRAC-tor
   D. LIZ-ard

4. **C**
   A. DOC-u-ment
   B. OP-tion-al
   C. ob-NOX-ious
   D. EN-er-gy

5. **D**
   A. em-PLOY-er
   B. con-TRIB-ute
   C. as-SIGN-ment
   D. SCAV-en-ger

6. **C**
   A. en-JOY-ment
   B. nu-TRI-tious
   C. HY-dro-gen
   D. em-BRACE-ment

7. **A**
   A. BA-ker
   B. cos-MET-ic
   C. in-FEC-tion
   D. ap-PLI-ance

8. **B**
   A. FA-vor-ite
   B. es-TAB-lish
   C. EX-cel-lence
   D. GLAM-or-ous

9. **D**
   A. PO-et-ry
   B. CRAN-ber-ry
   C. EX-cel-lence
   D. en-JOY-ment

10. **A**
    A. graf-FI-ti
    B. IN-dus-try
    C. TRIV-i-al
    D. LAV-en-der

11. **B**
    A. a-GREE-ment
    B. im-ma-TURE
    C. ad-VAN-tage
    D. re-CY-cle

12. **C**
    A. MA-ni-ac
    B. MEL-o-dy
    C. mi-GRA-tion
    D. ME-te-or

13. **A**
    A. vol-un-TEER
    B. WON-der-ful

C. HOR-ri-fy
D. MEM-ber-ship

14. **D**
    A. HU-mor-ous
    B. MES-sen-ger
    C. DIF-fer-ence
    D. mag-NET-ic

15. **B**
    A. HAND-i-cap
    B. com-PLEX-ion
    C. PHAR-ma-cy
    D. PED-es-tal

16. **B**
    A. VOL-un-tar-y
    B. tech-NOL-o-gy
    C. SEC-re-tar-y
    D. MIL-i-tar-y

17. **D**
    A. vi-o-LA-tion
    B. ce-le-BRA-tion
    C. gen-er-A-tion
    D. a-QUAR-i-um

18. **C**
    A. pro-FES-sion-al
    B. ad-VER-si-ty
    C. WA-ter-mel-on
    D. bel-LI-ger-ent

19. **C**
    A. ob-li-GA-tion
    B. pop-u-LA-tion
    C. pho-TOG-ra-phy
    D. car-o-LI-na

20. **A**
    A. de-GEN-er-ate
    B. DIC-tio-nar-y
    C. OR-di-nar-y
    D. BOD-y-buil-ding

21. **B**
    A. en-ter-TAIN-ment
    B. ant-ARC-ti-ca
    C. per-spi-RA-tion
    D. ed-u-CA-tion

22. **A**
    A. re-TI-re-ment
    B. LIT-er-a-ture
    C. TE-le-vi-sion
    D. AG-ri-cul-ture

23. **D**
    A. OB-vi-ous-ly
    B. AL-li-ga-tor
    C. NEC-es-sar-y
    D. in-TEG-ri-ty

24. **A**
    A. per-se-CU-tion
    B. di-REC-to-ry
    C. re-LA-tion-ship
    D. ca-NA-di-an

25. **C**
    A. a-NON-y-mous
    B. com-MU-ni-ty
    C. ter-mi-NA-tion
    D. so-CI-e-ty

26. **D**
    A. MAN-da-to-ry
    B. AR-chi-tec-ture

C. HE-li-cop-ter
D. de-LIV-er-y

27. **C**
    A. prep-o-SI-tion
    B. ev-er-LAST-ing
    C. de-MOC-ra-cy
    D. re-lax-A-tion

28. **B**
    A. al-TER-na-tive
    B. in-for-MA-tion
    C. e-TER-ni-ty
    D. an-XI-et-y

29. **B**
    A. in-de-PEN-dence
    B. po-TAS-si-um
    C. bu-reau-CRAT-ic
    D. dis-es-TAB-lish

30. **A**
    A. CIR-cu-la-tor-y
    B. com-MU-ni-cat-or
    C. vo-CAB-u-lar-y
    D. an-TIC-i-pat-ed

31. **D**
    A. ex-e-CU-tion-er
    B. gen-er-OS-it-y
    C. cu-ri-OS-it-y
    D. ad-MIN-is-tra-tor

32. **D**
    A. an-ni-VER-sa-ry
    B. so-ci-OL-o-gy
    C. bi-o-LOG-i-cal
    D. ex-TRAOR-di-nar-y

33. **B**
    A. or-ga-ni-ZA-tion
    B. caf-e-TE-ri-a
    C. e-lim-i-NA-tion
    D. par-tic-i-PA-tion

34. **C**
    A. ram-i-fi-CA-tion
    B. math-e-ma-TI-cian
    C. un-der-STAN-da-ble
    D. in-tox-i-CA-tion

35. **D**
    A. Par-al-LEL-o-gram
    B. per-pen-DIC-u-lar
    C. in-tel-LEC-tu-al
    D. clas-si-fi-CA-tion

36. **A**
    A. hos-pi-TAL-it-y
    B. de-gen-er-A-tion
    C. e-vap-o-RA-tion
    D. lou-i-si-AN-a

37. **C**
    A. ra-di-o-AC-tive
    B. glob-al-i-ZA-tion
    C. un-i-DEN-ti-fied
    D. pro-cra-sti-NA-tion

38. **B**
    A. di-a-BOL-i-cal
    B. an-tic-i-PA-tion
    C. in-fi-DEL-i-ty
    D. cre-a-TIV-i-ty

39. **C**
    A. as-tro-NOM-i-cal
    B. pop-u-LAR-i-ty

C. com-mu-ni-CA-tion
D. per-son-AL-i-ty

40. **D**
   A. ex-e-CU-tion
   B. in-de-CI-sive
   C. un-de-NI-able
   D. RA-tio-nal-ize

41. **A**
   A. per-son-i-fi-CA-tion
   B. de-ni-a-BIL-i-ty
   C. ac-cel-er-OM-e-ter
   D. in-vol-un-TAR-i-ly

42. **A**
   A. rev-o-LU-tion-ary
   B. re-spon-si-BIL-i-ty
   C. i-den-ti-FI-a-ble
   D. ex-tra-ter-RES-tri-al

43. **D**
   A. en-cy-clo-PE-di-a
   B. bi-o-di-VER-si-ty
   C. mem-o-ra-BIL-i-a
   D. spe-CIF-i-cal-ly

44. **A**
   A. i-den-ti-fi-CA-tion
   B. in-vol-un-TAR-i-ly
   C. di-vi-si-BIL-i-ty
   D. bi-o-tech-NOL-o-gy

45. **D**
   A. au-to-bi-OG-ra-phy
   B. bi-o-de-GRA-da-ble
   C. a-dap-ta-BIL-i-ty
   D. un-i-MAG-in-a-ble

46. C
   A. Breaks rule 3
   B. Breaks rule 2
   C. Correct
   D. Breaks rule 2 and 3

47. A
   A. Correct
   B. Breaks rule 1 and 3
   C. Breaks rule 1
   D. Breaks rule 2

48. B
   A. Breaks rule 2 and 3
   B. Correct
   C. Breaks rule 2
   D. Breaks rule 3

49. D
   A. Breaks rule 3
   B. Breaks rule 2
   C. Breaks rule 2
   D. Correct

50. C
   A. Breaks rule 1
   B. Breaks rule 2
   C. Correct
   D. Breaks rule 1

51. B
   A. Breaks rule 3
   B. Correct
   C. Breaks rule 1
   D. Breaks rule 2

52. A
   A. Correct
   B. Breaks rule 3

C. Breaks rule 1
D. Breaks rule 3

53. **D**
    A. Breaks rule 3
    B. Breaks rule 1 and 3
    C. Breaks rule 2
    D. Correct

54. **B**
    A. Breaks rule 2
    B. Correct
    C. Breaks rule 3
    D. Breaks rule 1

55. **D**
    A. Breaks rule 3
    B. Breaks rule 1
    C. Breaks rule 2
    D. Correct

56. **B**
    A. Breaks rule 2
    B. Correct
    C. Breaks rule 1
    D. Breaks rule 3

57. **A**
    A. Correct
    B. Breaks rule 3
    C. Breaks rule 2
    D. Breaks rule 2

58. **B**
    A. Breaks rule 1
    B. Correct
    C. Breaks rule 2
    D. Breaks rule 3

59. C
   A. Breaks rule 3
   B. Breaks rule 1
   C. Correct
   D. Breaks rule 3

60. A
   A. Correct
   B. Breaks rule 2 and 3
   C. Breaks rule 1
   D. Breaks rule 3

61. B
   A. Breaks rule 3
   B. Correct
   C. Breaks rule 2
   D. Breaks rule 1 and 2

62. A
   A. Correct
   B. Breaks rule 1
   C. Breaks rule 3
   D. Breaks rule 2 and 3

63. D
   A. Breaks rule 1 and 2
   B. Breaks rule 2 and 3
   C. Breaks rule 2
   D. Correct

64. C
   A. Breaks rule 1 and 3
   B. Breaks rule 1 and 2
   C. Correct
   D. Breaks rule 1

65. B
   A. Breaks rule 1
   B. Correct

C. Breaks rule 2
D. Breaks rule 3

66. C
  A. Breaks rule 4
  B. Breaks rule 6
  C. Correct
  D. Breaks rule 5

67. B
  A. Breaks rule 6
  B. Correct
  C. Breaks rule 6
  D. Breaks rule 4

68. A
  A. Correct
  B. Breaks rule 6
  C. Breaks rule 5
  D. Breaks rule 4

69. D
  A. Breaks rule 5
  B. Breaks rule 4 and 5
  C. Breaks rule 5
  D. Correct

70. B
  A. Breaks rule 5
  B. Correct
  C. Breaks rule 4, and 5
  D. Breaks rule 5 and 6

71. D

  A. Breaks rule 5
  B. Breaks rule 4
  C. Breaks rule 4
  D. Correct

72. **A**

   A. Correct
   B. Breaks rule 5
   C. Breaks rule 6
   D. Breaks rule 4

73. **B**

   A. Breaks rule 4 and 6
   B. Correct
   C. Breaks rule 5
   D. Breaks rule 5 and 6

74. **A**

   A. Correct
   B. Breaks rule 4, 5, and 6
   C. Breaks rule 4
   D. Breaks rule 4

75. **D**

   A. Breaks rule 5
   B. Breaks rule 4 and 5
   C. Breaks rule 4
   D. Correct

76. **C**

   A. Breaks rule 5
   B. Breaks rule 6
   C. Correct
   D. Breaks rule 5

77. **D**

   A. Breaks rule 5
   B. Breaks rule 5 and 6
   C. Breaks rule 5 and 6
   D. Correct

78. **A**

    A. Correct
    B. Breaks rule 5 and 6
    C. Breaks rule 6
    D. Breaks rule 4

79. **A**

    A. Correct
    B. Breaks rule 5
    C. Breaks rule 5
    D. Breaks rule 5

80. **C**

    A. Breaks rule 4
    B. Breaks rule 4 and 5
    C. Correct
    D. Breaks rule 5

81. **C**

    A. Breaks rule 4
    B. Breaks rule 4
    C. Correct
    D. Breaks rule 6

82. **D**

    A. Breaks rule 4
    B. Breaks rule 5 and 6
    C. Breaks rule 5
    D. Correct

83. **D**

    A. Breaks rule 5
    B. Breaks rule 5 and 6
    C. Breaks rule 5
    D. Correct

84. **A**

   A.   Correct
   B.   Breaks rule 5 and 6
   C.   Breaks rule 5 and 6
   D.   Breaks rule 6

85. **B**

   A.   Breaks rule 5 and 6
   B.   Correct
   C.   Breaks rule 4 and 5
   D.   Breaks rule 5

86. **D**

   A.   Breaks rule 5 and 6
   B.   Breaks rule5
   C.   Breaks rule 5 and 6
   D.   Correct

87. **B**

   A.   Breaks rule 4, 5 and 6
   B.   Correct
   C.   Breaks rule 4
   D.   Breaks rule 5 and 6

88. **C**

   A.   Breaks rule 7
   B.   Breaks rule 7
   C.   Correct
   D.   Breaks rule 9

89. **B**

   A.   Breaks rule 7
   B.   Correct
   C.   Breaks rule 7
   D.   Breaks rule 8

90. D

    A.   Breaks rule 9
    B.   Breaks rule 7
    C.   Breaks rule 7
    D. Correct

91. D

    A.   Breaks rule 8 and 9
    B.   Breaks rule 8 and 9
    C.   Breaks rule 7
    D.   Correct

92. B

    A.   Breaks rule 8
    B.   Correct
    C.   Breaks rule 7 and 8
    D.   Breaks rule 8

93. C

    A.   Breaks rule 7
    B.   Breaks rule 9
    C.   Correct
    D.   Breaks rule 9

94. A

    A.   Correct
    B.   Breaks rule 7
    C.   Breaks rule 8
    D.   Breaks rule 8

95. B

    A.   Breaks rule 7
    B.   Correct
    C.   Breaks rule 9
    D.   Breaks rule 7 and 8

96. D

    A.   Breaks rule 7
    B.   Breaks rule 8 and 9
    C.   Breaks rule 8 and 9
    D.   Correct

97. A

    A.   Correct
    B.   Breaks rule 8 and 9
    C.   Breaks rule 8
    D.   Breaks rule 7

98. C

    A.   Breaks rule 8 and 9
    B.   Breaks rule 8 and 9
    C.   Correct
    D.   Breaks rule 8

99. D

    A.   Breaks rule 7
    B.   Breaks rule 7 and 9
    C.   Breaks rule 9
    D.   Correct

100. C

    A.   Breaks rule 8 and 9
    B.   Breaks rule 7
    C.   Correct
    D.   Breaks rule 7

101. A

    A.   Correct
    B.   Breaks rule 9
    C.   Breaks rule 7
    D.   Breaks rule 8

102. A

   A. Correct
   B. Breaks rule 7
   C. Breaks rule 8 and 9
   D. Breaks rule 7

103. B

   A. Breaks rule 8 and 9
   B. Correct
   C. Breaks rule 7
   D. Breaks rule 8

104. D

   A. Breaks rule 7 and 8
   B. Breaks rule 9
   C. Breaks rule 8
   D. Correct

105. A

   A. Correct
   B. Breaks rule 9
   C. Breaks rule 8 and 9
   D. Breaks rule 8

106. A

   A. Correct
   B. Breaks rule 7
   C. Breaks rule 8 and 9
   D. Breaks rule 9

107. B

   A. Breaks rule 9
   B. Correct
   C. Breaks rule 7
   D. Breaks rule 8

108. C

    A.   Breaks rule 8 and 9
    B.   Breaks rule 8 and 9
    C.   Correct
    D.   Breaks rule 9

109. D

    A.   Breaks rule 7
    B.   Breaks rule 7 and 8
    C.   Breaks rule 7, 8, and 9
    D.   Correct

110. C

    A.   Breaks rule 1, 7, and 9
    B.   Breaks rule 7 and 9
    C.   Correct
    D.   Breaks rule 9

111. B

    A.   Breaks rule 1 and 8
    B.   Correct
    C.   Breaks rule 2
    D.   Breaks rule 3

112. B

    A.   Breaks rule 2 and 3
    B.   Correct
    C.   Breaks rule 2
    D.   Breaks rule 8

113. A

    A.   Correct
    B.   Breaks rule 3
    C.   Breaks rule 1 and 3
    D.   Breaks rule 8 and 9

114. A

    A. Correct
    B. Breaks rule 2 and 6
    C. Breaks rule 3 and 6
    D. Breaks rule 4 and 5

115. B

    A. Breaks rule 3 and 9
    B. Correct
    C. Breaks rule 2
    D. Breaks rule 2 and 3

116. D

    A. Breaks rule 1 and 2
    B. Breaks rule 3
    C. Breaks rule 2
    D. Correct

117. C

    A. Breaks rule 3
    B. Breaks rule 2 and 3
    C. Correct
    D. Breaks rule 2

118. C

    A. Breaks rule 9
    B. Breaks rule 8
    C. Correct
    D. Breaks rule 7

119. A

    A. Correct
    B. Breaks rule 2 and 7
    C. Breaks rule 1, 2, 3, and 7
    D. Breaks rule 3

120. C

    A. Breaks rule 4 and 5
    B. Breaks rule 4
    C. Correct
    D. Breaks rule 6

121. A

    A. Correct
    B. Breaks rule 2
    C. Breaks rule 3 and 4
    D. Breaks rule 4 and 5

122. D

    A. Breaks rule 2, 3, and 8
    B. Breaks rule 2, 3, and 8
    C. Breaks rule 2, 3, and 8
    D. Correct

123. A

    A. Correct
    B. Breaks rule 7
    C. Breaks rule 1
    D. Breaks rule 2 and 3

124. A

    A. Correct
    B. Breaks rule 4
    C. Breaks rule 1
    D. Breaks rule 4, 5, and 6

125. D

    A. Breaks rule 8
    B. Breaks rule 1
    C. Breaks rule 8
    D. Correct

126. C

    A.   Breaks rule 4
    B.   Breaks rule 2, 5, and 6
    C.   Correct
    D.   Breaks rule 3, 4 and 6

127. B

    A.   Breaks rule 3
    B.   Correct
    C.   Breaks rule 2 and 3
    D.   Breaks rule 2

128. B

    A.   Breaks rule 2
    B.   Correct
    C.   Breaks rule 2
    D.   Breaks rule 7

129. C

    A.   Breaks rule 1
    B.   Breaks rule 2
    C.   Correct
    D.   Breaks rule 3

130. A

    A.   Correct
    B.   Breaks rule 2B
    C.   Breaks rule 1B
    D.   Breaks rule 1B

131. B

    A.   Breaks 1B and 3B
    B.   Correct
    C.   Breaks 1B and 3B
    D.   Breaks rule 2B

132. C

    A.   Breaks rule 3B
    B.   Breaks rule 2B
    C.   Correct
    D.   Breaks rule 3B

133. D

    A.   Breaks rule 3B
    B.   Breaks rule 1B
    C.   Breaks rule 1B
    D.   Correct

134. C

    A.   Breaks rule 1B
    B.   Breaks rule 2B
    C.   Correct
    D.   Breaks rule 3B

135. A

    A.   Correct
    B.   Breaks rule 3B
    C.   Breaks rule 2B
    D.   Breaks rule 2B

136. B

    A.   Breaks rule 1B
    B.   Correct
    C.   Breaks rule 3B
    D.   Breaks rule 2B and 3B

137. D

    A.   Breaks rule 1B
    B.   Breaks rule 3B
    C.   Breaks rule 2B and 3B
    D.   Correct

138. B

    A.   Breaks rule 2B and 3B
    B.   Correct
    C.   Breaks rule 3B
    D.   Breaks rule 1B and 2B

139. D

    A.   Breaks rule 1B
    B.   Breaks rule 3B
    C.   Breaks rule 3B
    D.   Correct

140. B

    A.   Breaks rule 1B
    B.   Correct
    C.   Breaks rule 2B
    D.   Breaks rule 3B

141. C

    A.   Breaks rule 1B
    B.   Breaks rule 2B
    C.   Correct
    D.   Breaks rule 3B

142. D

    A.   Breaks rule 1B and 2B
    B.   Breaks rule 1B
    C.   Breaks rule 3B
    D.   Correct

143. D

    A.   Breaks rule 1B
    B.   Breaks rule 3B
    C.   Breaks rule 2B and 3B
    D.   Correct

144. A

    A. Correct
    B. Breaks rule 3B
    C. Breaks rule 1B
    D. Breaks rule 3B

145.

    A. Breaks rule 3B
    B. Correct
    C. Breaks rule 2B
    D. Breaks rule 1B

146. B

    A. Breaks rule 2B and 3B
    B. Correct
    C. Breaks rule 2B and 3B
    D. Breaks rule 1B

147. C

    A. Breaks rule 3B
    B. Breaks rule 2B
    C. Correct
    D. Breaks rule 2B and 3B

148. A

    A. Correct
    B. Breaks rule 2B and 3B
    C. Breaks rule 3B
    D. Breaks rule 2B

149. A

    A. Correct
    B. Breaks rule 3B
    C. Breaks rule 1B
    D. Breaks rule 2B

150. C

    A.   Breaks rule 5B
    B.   Breaks rule 4B
    C.   Correct
    D.   Breaks rule 6B

151. B

    A.   Breaks rule 5B and 6B
    B.   Correct
    C.   Breaks rule 4B, 5B, and 6B
    D.   Breaks rule 4B

152. D

    A.   Breaks rule 5B and 6B
    B.   Breaks rule 4B
    C.   Breaks rule 5B and 6B
    D.   Correct

153. C

    A.   Breaks rule 6B
    B.   Breaks rule 6B
    C.   Correct
    D.   Breaks rule 5B

154. A

    A.   Correct
    B.   Breaks rule 5B
    C.   Breaks rule 5B and 6B
    D.   Breaks rule 6B

155. C

    A.   Breaks rule 5B
    B.   Breaks rule 6B
    C.   Correct
    D.   Breaks rule 4B

156. B

- A. Breaks rule 5B and 6B
- B. Correct
- C. Breaks rule 4B and 5B
- D. Breaks rule 4B, 5B, and 6B

157. A

- A. Correct
- B. Breaks rule 5B and 6B
- C. Breaks rule 5B
- D. Breaks rule 6B

158. C

- A. Breaks rule 4B, 5B, and 6B
- B. Breaks rule 6B
- C. Correct
- D. Breaks rule 4B

159. B

- A. Breaks rule 4B
- B. Correct
- C. Breaks rule 4B, 5B, and 6B
- D. Breaks rule 6B

160. C

- A. Breaks rule 5B
- B. Breaks rule 4B, 5B, and 6B
- C. Correct
- D. Breaks rule 6B

161. C

- A. Breaks rule 6B
- B. Breaks rule 4B
- C. Correct
- D. Breaks rule 5B

162. B

    A. Breaks rule 5B
    B. Correct
    C. Breaks rule 4B, 5B, and 6B
    D. Breaks rule 4B

163. A

    A. Correct
    B. Breaks rule 5B and 6B
    C. Breaks rule 5B
    D. Breaks rule 4B

164. D

    A. Breaks rule 5B
    B. Breaks rule 6B
    C. Breaks rule 4B, 5B, and 6B
    D. Correct

165. C

    A. Breaks rule 4B
    B. Breaks rule 5B
    C. Correct
    D. Breaks rule 4B and 6B

166. B

    A. Breaks rule 5B and 6B
    B. Correct
    C. Breaks rule 4B
    D. Breaks rule 4B and 5B

167. D

    A. Breaks rule 5B and 6B
    B. Breaks rule 4B
    C. Breaks rule 4B, 5B, and 6B
    D. Correct

168. B

    A. Breaks rule 5B and 6B
    B. Correct
    C. Breaks rule 6B
    D. Breaks rule 4B

169. D

    A. Breaks rule 5B
    B. Breaks rule 5B and 6B
    C. Breaks rule 4B
    D. Correct

170. A

    A. Correct
    B. Breaks rule 4B
    C. Breaks rule 4B and 5B
    D. Breaks rule 6B

171. C

    A. Breaks rule 5B and 6B
    B. Breaks rule 4B and 5B
    C. Correct
    D. Breaks rule 4B

172. B

    A. Breaks rule 7B and 8B
    B. Correct
    C. Breaks rule 8B
    D. Breaks rule 9B

173. A

    A. Correct
    B. Breaks rule 7B
    C. Breaks rule 7B
    D. Breaks rule 9B

174. D

   A.   Breaks rule 7B
   B.   Breaks rule 9B
   C.   Breaks rule 8B
   D.   Correct

175. A

   A.   Correct
   B.   Breaks rule 8B
   C.   Breaks rule 7B
   D.   Breaks rule 9B

176. B

   A.   Breaks rule 7B
   B.   Correct
   C.   Breaks rule 9B
   D.   Breaks rule 8B

177. D

   A.   Breaks rule 9B
   B.   Breaks rule 8B
   C.   Breaks rule 7B
   D.   Correct

178. C

   A.   Breaks rule 7B and 8B
   B.   Breaks rule 8B
   C.   Correct
   D.   Breaks rule 9B

179. D

   A.   Breaks rule 8B
   B.   Breaks rule 8B
   C.   Breaks rule 9B
   D.   Correct

180. A

    A. Correct
    B. Breaks rule 7B and 8B
    C. Breaks rule 7B and 9B
    D. Breaks rule 7B

181. C

    A. Breaks rule 8B
    B. Breaks rule 8B
    C. Correct
    D. Breaks rule 9B

182. A

    A. Correct
    B. Breaks rule 8B
    C. Breaks rule 9B
    D. Breaks rule 9B

183. B

    A. Breaks rule 8B
    B. Correct
    C. Breaks rule 8B
    D. Breaks rule 7B

184. C

    A. Breaks rule 8B
    B. Breaks rule 7B, 8B, and 9B
    C. Correct
    D. Breaks rule 8B

185. A

    A. Correct
    B. Breaks rule 8B
    C. Breaks rule 8B and 9B
    D. Breaks rule 8B and 9B

186. A

    A.   Correct
    B.   Breaks rule 8B
    C.   Breaks rule 8B and 9B
    D.   Breaks rule 7B

187. D

    A.   Breaks rule 7B
    B.   Breaks rule 9B
    C.   Breaks rule 8B
    D.   Correct

188. D

    A.   Breaks rule 8B
    B.   Breaks rule 9B
    C.   Breaks rule 9B
    D.   Correct

189. A

    A.   Correct
    B.   Breaks rule 7B and 9B
    C.   Breaks rule 9B
    D.   Breaks rule 8B

190. B

    A.   Breaks rule 7B, 8B, and 9B
    B.   Correct
    C.   Breaks rule 9B
    D.   Breaks rule 8B

191. B

    A.   Breaks rule 9B
    B.   Correct
    C.   Breaks rule 8B
    D.   Breaks rule 9B

192. A

    A.   Correct
    B.   Breaks rule 8B
    C.   Breaks rule 8B and 9B
    D.   Breaks rule 9B

193. C

    A.   Breaks rule 7B
    B.   Breaks rule 9B
    C.   Correct
    D.   Breaks rule 8B

194. D

    A.   Breaks rule 7B and 8B
    B.   Breaks rule 1B
    C.   Breaks rule 8B
    D.   Correct

195. A

    A.   Correct
    B.   Breaks rule 8B
    C.   Breaks rule 1B
    D.   Breaks rule 9B

196. A

    A.   Correct
    B.   Breaks rule 5B and 6B
    C.   Breaks rule 5B and 6B
    D.   Breaks rule 4B and 5B

197. B

    A.   Breaks rule 3B
    B.   Correct
    C.   Breaks rule 3B and 9B
    D.   Breaks rule 9B

198. C

    A.   Breaks rule 1B
    B.   Breaks rule 2B and 3B
    C.   Correct
    D.   Breaks rule 7B

199. D

    A.   Breaks rule 2B
    B.   Breaks rule 2B
    C.   Breaks rule 2B and 3B
    D.   Correct

200. D

    A.   Breaks rule 4B, 6B, and 9B
    B.   Breaks rule 9B
    C.   Breaks rule 5B
    D.   Correct

201. B

    A.   Breaks rule 2B and 3B
    B.   Correct
    C.   Breaks rule 2B
    D.   Breaks rule 1B and 8B

202. A

    A.   Correct
    B.   Breaks rule 7B
    C.   Breaks rule 1B
    D.   Breaks rule 7B

203. B

    A.   Breaks rule 2B and 3B
    B.   Correct
    C.   Breaks rule 2B
    D.   Breaks rule 7B.

204. C

- A. Breaks rule 9B
- B. Breaks rule 9B
- C. Correct
- D. Breaks rule 7B

205. C

- A. Breaks rule 3B
- B. Breaks rule 2B, 7B, and 9B
- C. Correct
- D. Breaks rule 1B and 8B

206. A

- A. Correct
- B. Breaks rule 3B and 7B
- C. Breaks rule 2B
- D. Breaks rule 2B, 3B and 9B

207. A

- A. Correct
- B. Breaks rule 5B and 9B
- C. Breaks rule 4B and 6B
- D. Breaks rule 5B and 6B

208. D

- A. Breaks rule 7B and 9B
- B. Breaks rule 1B
- C. Breaks rule 7B
- D. Correct

209. B

- A. Breaks rule 3B
- B. Correct
- C. Breaks rule 2B
- D. Breaks rule 1B

210. B

    A. Breaks rule 3B
    B. Correct
    C. Breaks rule 2B and 3B
    D. Breaks rule 1B and 3B

211. D

    A. Breaks rule 8B
    B. Breaks rule 8B
    C. Breaks rule 9B
    D. Correct

212. A

    A. Correct
    B. Breaks rule 2B
    C. Breaks rule 1B
    D. Breaks rule 3B

213. C

    A. Breaks rule 1B
    B. Breaks rule 4B
    C. Correct
    D. Breaks rule 4B and 5B

214. A

    A. Correct: The image is of a dolphin. The dolphin and fish are most similar. The beginning contains "sea" as shown for the dolphin
    B. Ending contains "tion" as shown for cat
    C. Ending contains "ardo" as shown for the bird
    D. Beginning contains "eg" as shown for the bird

215. B

    A. Beginning contains "Le" as shown for the insect and the ending contains "tion" as shown for the cat
    B. Correct: An airplane and bird are most similar. Ending contains "ardo" as shown for bird

C. Beginning contains "se" as shown for the dolphin and the ending contains "on" as shown for the cat

D. Beginning contains "cat" as shown for cat and the ending contains "ly" as shown for the dolphin

216. A

A. Correct: The image is a flying insect and therefore the ant and bird are most similar. Beginning contains "le" as shown for the ant and the ending contains "ardo" as shown for the bird

B. Beginning contains "sea" as shown for the dolphin and the ending contains "do" as shown for the bird

C. Ending contains "tion" as shown for the cat

D. Ending contains "ly" as shown for the dolphin

217. D

A. Ending contains "ic" as shown for the deer and the beginning contains "ket" as shown for the ending of the fish

B. Beginning contains "dor" as shown for the deer

C. Beginning contains "tion" as shown for the ending of cat and the ending contains "er" as shown for the ending of the chair

D. Correct: The cat and deer are most similar to the cat chasing the deer. Beginning contains "cat" as shown for the cat and the ending contains "ic" as shown for the deer.

218. B

A. No words are similar

B. Correct: A cat sitting and reading on a chair is most similar to the chair and the cat. Beginning contains "lev" as shown for the chair and the ending contains "tion" as shown for the cat

C. Ending contains "tion" as shown for just the cat

D. Ending contains "oric" as shown for the deer

219. B

A. No words are similar

B. Correct: The fish is similar to the other fish. Ending contains "ket" as shown for the other fish

C. Beginning contains "do" as shown for the deer and the ending contains "ver" as shown for the chair

D. No words are similar

220. C

A. No words are similar
B. Beginning contains "mar" as shown for the dancer and the ending contains "ress" as shown for the bike
C. Correct: The girl holding the balloons is most similar to the balloon sine they both contain balloons. Beginning contains "le" as shown for the balloon
D. Beginning contains "cu" as shown for the couple and the ending contains "ance" as shown for the dancer

221. A

A. Correct: The couple biking is most similar to the bike and the couple. The beginning contains "cu" as shown for the couple and the ending contains "ress" as shown for the bike
B. Beginning contains "le" as shown for the balloon and the ending contains "rance" as shown for the dancer
C. Beginning contains "ana" as shown for the bike
D. Ending contains "ant" as shown for the balloon

222. D

A. Ending contains "mar" which is at the beginning of dance
B. Beginning contains "ana" as shown for the bike and the ending contains "cu" as shown for the beginning of the couple
C. A "v" has been added to the word as shown for dance
D. Correct: The couple and the dancer are most similar to the couple dancing. The beginning contains "mar"as shown for the dancer and the ending contains "ity" for the couple

223. C

A. Beginning contains "co" as shown for the woman playing tennis and the ending contains "low" as shown for the man on the phone.
B. Beginning contains "et" as shown for the cello and the ending contains "rect" as shown for the soccer ball
C. Correct: The image is a woman playing soccer. The woman playing tennis and soccer ball are most similar. Beginning contains "ro" for the soccer ball and the ending contains "hip" for the tennis player

D. Beginning contains "hip" as shown for the woman playing tennis and the ending contains "low" as shown for the man on the phone

224. B

A. Beginning contains "ent" as shown for the man on the phone and the end contains "rite" as shown for the cello

B. Correct: The image is a woman playing the cello. The women playing tennis and the cello have the most in common. The beginning contains "co" as shown in the woman playing tennis and the ending contains "rite" as shown for the cello *

C. Beginning contains "et" as shown for the cello and the ending contains "rect" as shown for the soccer ball

D. Beginning contains "et" as shown for the cello and the ending contains "low" as shown for the man on the phone

225. A

A. Correct: The image shows a man playing a violin. The image of the man on the phone and the cello are most similar. Beginning contains "ent" for the man on the phone and the ending contains "rite" for the cello

B. Beginning contains "co" as show for the woman playing tennis and the ending contains "rite" as shown for the cello

C. Beginning contains "et" as shown for the cello and the ending contains "hip" as shown for the woman playing tennis

D. Beginning contains "ent" as shown for the man on the phone and the ending contains "rect" as shown for the soccer ball

226. B

A. Beginning contains "ban" as shown for the plane and the ending contains "crow" as shown for the chicken

B. Correct: The image is of 5 chickens. Therefore, the image of the chicken and the number 5 are most similar. Beginning contains "bel" as shown for the chicken and the ending contains "vo" as shown for #5

C. Beginning contains "re' as shown for #5 and the ending contains "tish" as shown for the plane

D. Beginning contains "re" as shown for #5 and the ending contains "ina" as shown for the pig

227. A

    A.   Correct: The image is a flying pig and therefore the plane and pig are most similar. Beginning contains "bant" as shown for the plane and the ending contains "tina" as shown for the pig

    B.   Beginning contains "bel" as shown for the chicken and the ending contains "tish" as shown for the plane

    C.   Beginning contains "vo" as shown for the ending of #5 and the ending contains "tina" as shown for the pig

    D.   Ending contains "vo" as shown for #5

228. A

    A.   Correct: The image is that of a goose flying which is most similar to the chicken and the plane. Beginning contains "bel" as shown for the chicken and the ending contains "tish" as shown for the plane

    B.   Beginning contains "ban" as shown for the plane and the ending contains "tina" as show for the pig

    C.   Beginning contains "tish" as shown for the ending of the plane and the ending contains "vo" as shown for #5

    D.   Beginning contains "le" as shown for the pig and the ending contains "crow" as shown for the chicken

229. D

    A.   No words are similar

    B.   Beginning contains "so" as shown for the swing and the ending contains "vo" as shown for #5

    C.   Beginning contains "let" as shown for the pig and the ending contains "ite" as shown for the box.

    D.   Correct: The image is a pig on a swing. The image of the pig and the swing are most similar. Beginning contains "lev" as shown for the pig and the ending contains "vil" as shown for the swing

230. C

    A.   Beginning contains "nan" as shown for the box and the ending contains "ina" as shown for the pig

    B.   Beginning contains "sov as shown for the swing and the ending contains "ite" as shown for the box

C.   Correct: The image shows 5 suitcases. The image of the box and #5 are most similar. The beginning contains "na" as shown for the box and the ending contains "vo" for #5

D.   The word is "revo" which is already shown for the #5

231. A

A.   Correct: The image shows a hand displaying 5 fingers. Only #5 is similar. The beginning contains "rev" as shown for #5 and no words are similar to the ending "lin"

B.   Ending contains "vil" as shown for the swing. No words are similar to the beginning "ro"

C.   Ending contains "ite" as shown for the box. No words are similar to the beginning "tor"

D.   Beginning contains "le" as shown for the pig and the ending contains "ite" as shown for the box

232. C

A.   Ending contains "ing" as shown for the three dots. No words are similar to the beginning "bar"

B.   No words are similar

C.   Correct: It is an oil barrel. The oil rig is most similar. The beginning contains "bes" for the oil rig and no words are similar to "rel"

D.   Ending contains "ern" as shown for the computer. No words are similar to the beginning "bus"

233. D

A.   Beginning contains "cin" as shown for the three dots. No words are similar to the ending "ol"

B.   Beginning contains "bes" as shown for the oil rig and the ending contains "age" as shown for the hurdler

C.   Ending contains "ern" as shown for the computer. No words are similar to the beginning "dol"

D.   Correct: The image shows 3 depictions of a man doing an activity. The hurdler and 3 dots are most similar. The beginning contains "dack" for the hurdler and the ending contains "ing" for the 3 dots

234. B

A.   Beginning contains "cu" as shown for the computer and the ending contains "es" as shown for the oil rig

B.   Correct: The image is that of a smartphone which is a mini computer. The image of the desktop computer is most similar.

The beginning contains "cu" as shown for the desktop computer. No words are similar to the ending "let"

C. Beginning contains "cu" as shown for the computer and the ending contains "ing" as shown for the three dots

D. Beginning contains "cu" as shown for the computer and the ending contains "age" as shown for the hurdler

235. A

A. Correct: The image is a pair of eyeglasses. The image of the eye is most similar. The ending contains "dox" as shown for the eye. No words are similar to the beginning "da"

B. Ending contains "gent" as shown for the shower. No words are similar to the beginning "pre"

C. No words are similar

D. Ending contains "gent" as shown for the shower. No words are similar to the beginning "ron"

236. D

A. Beginning contains "el" as shown for the three fingers and the ending contains "gent" as shown for the shower

B. Beginning contains "cle" as shown for the cleaning lady and the ending contains "and" as shown for the three fingers

C. Beginning contains "spon" as shown for the shower head and the ending contains "ox" as shown for the eye

D. Correct: The image is of an elephant cleaning itself in a bathtub. The beginning contains "cle" as shown for the cleaning lady and the ending contains "gent" as shown for the shower head

237. B

A. Ending contains "esk" as shown for the cleaning lady. No words are similar to the beginning "count"

B. Correct: The image is of 3 people. The image of the 3 fingers is most similar. The ending contains "vand" as shown for the three fingers. No words are similar to the beginning "rum"

C. No words are similar

D. Ending contains "gent" as shown for the showerhead. No words are similar to the beginning "va"

238. C

A. Beginning contains "nan" as shown for the box and the ending contains "ect" as shown for the ball

B. No words are similar

C. Correct: The image is of a jack in the box. The image of the box and the man are most similar. The beginning contains "nan" as shown for the box and the ending contains "tum" as shown for the man

D. Ending contains "ite" as shown for the box. No words are similar to the beginning containing "hil"

239. A

A. Correct: The image is of man playing an instrument. The image of the instruments and man are most similar. The beginning contains "ent" as shown for the man and the ending contains "mist" as shown for the instruments

B. Beginning contains "ro" as shown for the ball and the ending contains "um" as shown for the man.

C. Ending contains" ite" as shown for the box. No words are similar to the beginning containing "val"

D. Ending contains "um" as shown for the man. No words are similar to the beginning containing "rel"

240. C

A. No words are similar

B. No words are similar

C. Correct: The image is a circle inside a square. The image of the box and the ball are most similar The beginning contains "nan" as shown for the box and the ending contains "ect" as shown for the ball

D. No words are similar

241. D

A. Beginning contains "kar" as shown for the butterfly and the ending contains "ia" as shown for the glass

B. Beginning contains "eis" as shown for the dog and the ending contains "do" as shown for the butterfly

C. Beginning contains "kun" as shown for the glass and no words are similar to the ending "do"

D. Correct: The image is a musical note with wings. The musical note and butterfly are most similar. Beginning contains "kara" for the butterfly and the ending contains "dum" for the musical note

242. A

A. Correct: The image is that of a mug. The picture of the glass is most similar. The beginning contains "kun" as shown for the glass and no words are similar to the ending "sto"
B. Beginning contains "stra" as shown for the as shown for the music note. No words are similar to the ending "ly"
C. Ending contains "der" as shown for the dog. No words are similar to the beginning "mis"
D. Ending contains "do" as shown for the butterfly. No words are similar to the beginning "na"

243. C

A. Beginning contains "stra" as shown for the music note and the ending contains "er" as shown for the dog
B. Beginning contains "karad" as shown for the butterfly and the ending contains "er" as shown for the dog
C. Correct: The image is a hot dog. The dog is most similar. Beginning contains "eis" for the dog. No words are similar to "ing"
D. Beginning contains "Strad" as shown for the music note and the ending contains "er" as shown for the dog

244. D

A. Beginning contains "sa" as shown for the sail boat and the ending contains "dant" as shown for the fire
B. Beginning contains "cho" as shown for the shoe and the ending contains "por" as shown for the sail boat
C. Beginning contains "por" which is shown for the ending of the sail boat and the ending contains "ben" which is shown for the man
D. Correct: The image is of a man with a sailboat in a wheelbarrow. The man and sailboat are most similar. Beginning contains "sa" for the sail boat and the ending contains "ben" for the man

245. C

A. Beginning contains "cho" as shown for the shoe and the ending contains "dant" as shown for the fire
B. Beginning contains "du" as shown for the fire and the ending contains "por" as shown for the sail boat

C. Correct: The image is of a fire hydrant. The image of the fire is most similar. No words are similar to the beginning "sho" and the ending contains "dant" as shown for the fire

D. Ending contains "ben" as shown for the man and no words are similar to the beginning "row"

246. B

A. Beginning contains "du" as shown for the fire and the ending contains "nt" as also shown for the fire

B. Correct: The image is that of a footprint. The image of the shoe is most similar. The beginning contains "cho" as shown for the shoe and no words contain the ending "dar"

C. No words are similar

D. No words are similar

247. D

A. Ending contains "low" for the man. No words begin have "le"

B. Beginning contains "ent" as shown for the man and the ending contains "oll" as shown for the barber pole

C. No words are similar

D. Correct: The image is a fish with legs. The image of the man and fish are most similar. The beginning contains "lora" for the fish and the ending contains "low" for the man

248. A

A. Correct: The image is of a man on the phone. The images of the man and the phone are most similar. The beginning contains "kro" as shown for the phone and the ending contains "low" as shown for the man

B. Beginning contains "lor" as shown for the fish and the ending contains "one" as shown for the phone

C. Ending contains "roll" as shown for the barber pole

D. Beginning contains "ent" as shown for the man. No words are similar to the ending "ol"

249. B

A. Beginning contains "ent" as shown for the man and no words are similar to the ending "ol"

B. Correct: The image is a comb and scissors. The image of the barber pole is most similar. The beginning contains "bar" as shown for the barber pole. No words contain the ending "ly"

C. No words are similar

D. No words are similar

250. A

A. Correct: The image is a paintbrush. The paint can and the pencil are most similar. The beginning contains "ana' for the paint and the ending contains "di" for the pencil

B. Beginning contains "ana" as shown for the paint and the ending contains "loit" as shown for the fruit bowl

C. Beginning contains "ter" as shown for the basketball net and the ending contains "di" as shown for the pencil

D. Beginning contains "des" as shown for the fruit bowl and the ending contains "gate" as shown for the paint

251. C

A. Beginning contains "des" as shown for the fruit bowl and the ending contains "ix" as shown for the basketball net

B. Beginning contains "ana" as shown for the paint and the ending contains "loit" as shown for the fruit bowl

C. Correct: It is a man eating from a bowl. The fruit bowl is most similar. No words contain "fo" ending has "loit" for the fruit bowl

D. Beginning contains "cre" as shown for the pencil and the ending contains "loit" as shown for the fruit bowl

252. C

A. Beginning contains "cre" for the pencil. No words contain the ending "ter"

B. The beginning contains "des" as shown for the fruit bowl. No words contain the ending "ter"

C. Correct: The image is that of a spider web, the image of the basketball net is most similar. No words contain the beginning "sped" The ending contains "ix" as shown for the basketball net

D. Beginning contains 'cre" as shown for the pencil and the ending contains "ix" as shown for the basketball net

253. B

A. No words are similar
B. Correct: The image is of a coil of rope. The image of the snake coiled up is most similar. The middle of the word contains "cum" as shown in the image of the snake
C. No words are similar
D. No words are similar

254. A

A. Correct: The image is of an ambulance. The image of the van and the hospital are most similar. The beginning contains "ca" as shown for the hospital and the ending contains "po" as shown for the van
B. The beginning contains "ro" which is shown for the middle of the van and the ending contains "be" as shown for the horse
C. Beginning contains "so" as shown for the snake and the ending contains "be" as shown for the horse
D. No words are similar to the beginning "cu" and the ending contains "po" as shown for the van

255. D

A. No words are similar
B. The middle contains "be' as shown for the ending of the horse
C. The middle contains "so" as shown for the beginning of the snake
D. Correct: The image is of a horseshoe. The image of the horse is most similar. The middle contains "lan" as shown for the middle of the horse

256. B

A. Beginning contains "co" as shown for the van and the ending contains "lor" as shown for the book and graduation hat
B. Correct: the image is of a box truck. The image of the box and van are most similar. The beginning contains "cor" as shown for the van and the ending contains "nite" as shown for the box
C. Beginning contains "na" as shown for the box and the ending contains "lor" as shown for the book and graduation hat
D. Beginning contains "ent" as shown for the man and the ending contains "ite" as shown for the bike

257. A

A. Correct: The image is a stack of books. The image of the box and the book and hat are most similar. The beginning contains "na" for the box and the ending contains "lor" for the book and grad hat

B. Beginning contains "na" as shown for the box and the ending contains "low" as shown for the man

C. Ending contains "low" as shown for the man

D. No words are similar

258. C

A. No words are similar to the beginning and the ending contains "low" as shown for the man

B. No words are similar to the beginning. Ending contains "na' as shown for the beginning of the box

C. Correct: The image is of a man dragging a box. The image of the box and the man are most similar. The beginning contains "ent" for the man and the ending contains "ite" as shown for the box

D. No words are similar to the beginning. Ending contains "low" as shown for the image of the man

259. B

A. No words are similar to the beginning "re" and the ending contains "mozen" as shown for the boxers.

B. Correct: The image is of two sword fighters. The image of the sword and the boxers is most similar. The beginning contains "tr" as shown for the sword and the middle contains "moz" as shown for the middle of the boxers

C. No words are similar to the beginning and the ending contains "gic" as shown for the sword

D. No words are similar

260. A

A. Correct: The image is of two bears boxing. The image of the bear and the boxers is most similar. Beginning contains "di" as shown for the boxers and the ending contains "lin" as shown for the bear

B. Ending contains "zen" as shown for the image of the bear

C. Beginning contains "che" as show for the image of the bears, the middle contains "vid" as shown for the image of the film and the ending contains "ic" as shown for the image of the sword

D. Ending contains "in" as shown for the image of the bear

261. D

A. The beginning contains "em" as shown for the film and the ending contains "don" as shown for the film, but the middle contains "leg" as shown for the sword

B. No words are similar

C. Middle contains "ven" as shown for the film and the ending contains "en" as shown for the boxers

D. Correct: The image is of a movie board. The image of the film is most similar. Ending contains "don" as shown for the film

262. C

A. Beginning contains "pre as shown for the statue of liberty and the ending contains "tue" as shown for the statue of liberty but the middle contains "vil" as shown for the arm

B. Beginning contains "ana" as shown for the tire and the ending contains "tue" as shown for the statue of liberty

C. Correct: The image is of scale representing law/justice. The statue of liberty is most similar. Ending contains "tue" for the statue

D. Beginning contains "pre" as shown for the statue of liberty and the ending contains "len" as shown for the arm

263. A

A. Correct: the image is of man lifting weights. The image of the arm with muscle is most similar. Ending contains "vilen" for the arm

B. Beginning contains "mi" as shown for the arm and the ending contains "dud" as shown for the beginning of the fire

C. Middle contains "nar" as shown for the tire

D. Middle contains "len" as shown for the ending of the arm and the ending contains "mi" as shown for the beginning of the arm

264. C

A. Beginning contains "du" as shown for the fire and the ending contains "len" as shown for the arm

B. Beginning contains "an" for the tire and the ending contains "ess" for the tire, but the middle contains "vil" as shown for the muscle

C. Correct: The image is a tire on fire. The image of the fire and the tire are most similar. Beginning contains "du" for the fire and the middle contains "ar" for the tire

D. Ending contains "ess" as shown for the tire

265. B

A. Beginning contains "lo" as shown for the trombone and the ending contains "on" as shown for the cat

B. Correct: The image is a trumpet. The image of the trombone is most similar. The middle contains "cal" as shown for the middle of the trombone

C. Middle contains "mist" for the ending of the trombone

D. Middle contains "cal" as shown for the trumpet and the ending contains "on" as shown for the cat

266. A

A. Correct: The image is of a violin which is a string instrument. The image of the harp is most similar since it is also a string instrument. Ending contains "rite" as shown for the harp

B. Beginning contains "est" for the harp and the ending contains "lor" as shown for the man reading the newspaper

C. Beginning contains "lo" as shown for the trombone and the ending contains "rite" as shown for the harp

D. No words are similar

267. D

A. No words are similar

B. Ending contains "rite" as shown for the harp

C. Middle contains "lor" for the man reading a newspaper

D. Correct: The image is of a cat reading. The image of the cat and the man reading the newspaper are most similar. Beginning contains "the" as shown for the man reading and the ending contains "ion" as shown for the cat

268. B

A. Ending contains "rect" as shown for the soccer ball

B.   Correct: The image is of sunscreen. The image of the sun is most similar. Ending contains "cal" as shown for the sun
C.   No words are similar
D.   Ending contains "do" as shown for the barn

269. D

A.   Beginning contains "le" for the dragonfly and the middle contains "ro" as shown for the beginning of the soccer ball. Though the image pair is correct, the order is not.
B.   Beginning contains "ro" as shown for the soccer ball. The middle contains "lan" as shown for the middle of the dragon fly and the ending contains "al" as shown for the sun
C.   Beginning contains "ro" as shown for the soccer ball and the ending contains "do" as shown for the barn
D.   Correct: The image is of soccer ball with wings. The image of the dragonfly and the soccer ball are most similar. Middle contains "lan" as shown for the middle of the dragon fly and the ending contains "ect" as shown for the soccer ball

270. A

A.   Correct: The image is of a cow (farm animal) on top of cheese (round). The image of the barn and the round soccer ball is most similar. Beginning contains "cam" as shown for the barn and the ending contains "ect" as shown for the soccer ball
B.   Ending contains "ing" as shown for the dragon fly
C.   Middle contains "lan" as shown for the dragon fly and the ending contains "do" as shown for the barn
D.   Ending contains "ing" as shown for the dragon fly

271. D

A.   Ending contains "ess" as shown for the tires
B.   No words are similar
C.   Beginning contains "re" as shown for the cars colliding and the ending contains "chen" as shown for the dinosaur
D.   Correct: The image is of a broken down car. The image of the cars colliding is most similar. Middle contains "ra" as shown for the cars colliding

272. B

A. Beginning contains "le" as shown for the bee and the ending contains "any" as shown for the cars colliding
B. Correct: the image is of a dragon. The image of the dinosaur and the bee with wings are most similar. Middle contains "mec" as shown for the dinosaur and the ending contains "ing" as shown for the bee
C. Beginning contains "lo" as shown for the dinosaur, the middle contains "lan" as shown for the bee, but the ending contains "ess" as shown for the tires
D. Ending contains "en" as shown for the dinosaur

273. C

A. Ending contains "chen" as shown for the dinosaur
B. Beginning contains "re" as shown for the cars colliding
C. Correct: The image is of a two wheeled vehicle, a motorcycle. The image of the two tires is most similar. Middle contains "nar" as shown for the two tires
D. Ending contains "ing" as shown for the bee

274. A

A. Correct: The image is of a hand flicking a switch. The image of the lightbulb is most similar as it is the only image we can be turned on and off with a switch. Ending contains "ca" as shown for the light bulb
B. No words are similar
C. Ending contains "cal" as shown for the conversation bubbles
D. No words are similar

275. C

A. Ending contains "ben" as shown for the man
B. Beginning contains "bur" as shown for the keys and the ending contains "ca" as shown for the light bulb
C. Correct. The image is a doorknob with a lock. The image of the keys is most similar. Ending contains "rel" for the keys
D. Beginning contains "bro" as shown for the man and the ending contains "rel" as shown for the keys

276. B

A. Middle contains "cri" as shown for the beginning of the conversation bubbles
B. Correct: The image is of two men talking. The image of the man and the conversation bubbles are most similar. Beginning contains "bro" as shown for the man and the ending contains "al" as shown for the conversation bubbles
C. Ending contains "al" as shown for the conversation bubbles
D. Ending contains "cal" as shown for the conversation bubbles

277. D

A. Beginning contains "tro" as shown for the sword. The middle contains "mer" as shown for the bridge and the ending contains "ay" as shown for the bowl
B. Beginning contains "cle" as shown for the vacuum. The middle contains "ken" as shown for the end of the bridge and the ending contains "ic" as shown for the sword
C. Middle contains "tro" as shown for the beginning of the sword and the ending contains "ay" as shown for the bowl
D. Correct: The image is of a safety pin which has the pointy end visible. The image of the sword with its point is most similar. The ending contains "ic" as shown for the sword

278. B

A. Middle contains "mer" for the bridge and the ending contains "ay" as shown for the bowl
B. Correct: The image is the top of a pillar. The most similar image to construction and holding things up is the bridge. The ending contains "en" as shown for the bridge
C. Beginning contains "spo" as show for the bridge. The ending contains "legic" as shown for the sword
D. Ending contains "spo" as shown for the beginning of the bridge. Correct image pair but wrong order

279. D

A. No words are similar
B. Middle contains "mer" as shown for the bridge. The ending contains "ay" as shown for the bowl
C. Middle contains "leg" as shown for the sword

D. Correct: The image is of a man cleaning dishes. The image of the vacuum used for cleaning and the bowl are most similar. Beginning contains "cle" for the vacuum and the middle contains "lat" for the bowl

280. A

A. Correct: The image is of a spider. The image of the spider web is most similar. Ending contains "rix" as shown for the spider web
B. No words are similar
C. Ending contains "nest" as shown for the hour glass
D. Beginning contains "bul" as shown for the hour glass and the ending contains "rix" as shown for the web

281. C

A. Beginning contains "cli" as shown for the cow
B. Beginning contains "ro" as shown for the little bow and the ending contains "nest" as shown for the hour glass
C. Correct: The image is a cowboy. The image of the cow and the boy are most similar. Beginning contains "ro" for the boy and the ending contains "bo" as shown for the cow
D. Beginning contains "cli" as shown for the cow and the ending contains "rix" as shown for the spider web

282. B

A. Beginning contains "bul" as shown for the hour glass and the ending contains "bo" as shown for the cow
B. Correct: The image is a clock. The image of the hourglass, which keeps time, is most similar. Ending contains "est" as shown for the hour glass
C. No words are similar
D. Beginning contains "ter" for the spider web and the ending contains "bul" as shown for the beginning of the hour glass

283. D

A. Middle contains "ner" as shown for the grim reaper and the ending contains "ment" as shown for the rocket ship
B. Middle contains "ban" as shown for the beginning of the plane and the ending contains "ag' as shown for the grim reaper

C. Ending contains "en" as shown for the hammer

D. Correct: The image is a tombstone. The image of the grim reaper is most similar since it represents death. Ending contains "ag" for the grim reaper

284. A

A. Correct: The image is an anvil. The image of the hammer is most similar since they are used together. Ending contains "len" for the hammer

B. Beginning contains "ban" as shown for the plane

C. Beginning contains "sta" as shown for the hammer and the ending contains "tist" as shown for the middle of the rocket ship

D. No words are similar

285. C

A. Beginning contains "ast" as shown for the rocket ship. Middle contains "ner" as shown for the grim reaper and the ending contains "ish" as shown for the plane

B. Beginning contains "ast" as shown for the rocket ship. Middle contains "we" as shown for the hammer

C. Correct: The image is of a space shuttle, which is most similar to the rocket ship and plane. The beginning contains "ban" for the plane and the ending contains "ment" as shown for the rocket ship

D. Beginning contains "ban" as shown for the plane. Middle contains "rag" as shown for the ending of the grim reaper and the ending contains "ment" as shown for the rocket ship

286. B

A. Middle contains "in" as shown for the ending of the hand with dice and the ending contains "cal" as shown for the man on the horse

B. Correct: The image is of a royal on a horse. The image of the crown and the man on the horse are most similar. The beginning contains "fro" as shown for the crown and the ending contains "cal" as shown for the man on the horse

C. Beginning contains "no" as shown for the man on the horse and the ending contains "sive" as shown for the fox

D. Beginning contains "Sen" as shown for the fox and the ending contains "litber" as shown for the crown

287. A

    A. Correct: The image is a person riding a fox. The image of the fox and the man on the horse are most similar. Beginning contains "Sen" for the fox and the middle contains "vit" for the man on the horse

    B. Beginning contains "nov" as shown for the man on the horse. Middle contains "lit" as shown for the crown and the ending contains "min" as shown for the hand holding the dice

    C. Beginning contains "fro" as shown for the crown and the ending contains "ssive" as shown for the fox

    D. Ending contains "ive" as shown for the fox

288. D

    A. Beginning contains "bel" for the hand with dice. Middle contains "lit" for the crown. Ending contains "cal" for the man on the horse

    B. Middle contains "bel" as for the beginning of the hand with dice

    C. Middle contains "re" as shown for the fox

    D. Correct: The image shows a hand of cards similar to gambling. The hand holding the dice is most similar since it is associated with gambling. Ending contains "min" as for the hand with the dice

289. C

    A. No words are similar

    B. Beginning contains "sen" as shown for the fox. Middle contains "cra" as shown for the wagon and the ending contains "tard" as shown for the hat

    C. Correct: The image is of a fox with a top hat. The image of the fox and hat are most similar. Middle contains "vest" as shown for the hat and the ending contains "ive" as shown for the fox

    D. Beginning contains "du' as shown for the hat. Middle contains "cra" as shown for the wagon and the ending contains "ment" as shown for the camera

290. D

    A. No words are similar

    B. Ending contains "ment" as shown for the camera

    C. No words are similar

D. Correct: The image is of Santa and his deer. The image of the ˋ wagon is most similar since they are both being pulled by animals. Ending contains "dor" as shown for the wagon

291. B

A. Beginning contains "int" as for the wagon. Middle contains "ves" as for the hat and the ending contains "ssive" as shown for the fox
B. Correct: The Image is of a photogapher taking a picture. The image of the camera is most similar. The middle contains "mus" as shown for the camera
C. Beginning contains "re" as shown for the camera and the ending contains "dor" as shown for the wagon
D. Middle contains "mus" as shown for the camera and the ending contains "ard" as shown for the hat

292. A

A. Correct: The image is of a snail, which is a slow creature. The image that is most similar to the turtle, which is also slow. Ending contains "wen" as shown for the turtle
B. Beginning contains "man" as shown for the rabbit and the ending contains "er" as shown for the club
C. No words are similar
D. Beginning contains "che" as shown for the bear

293. B

A. Beginning contains "che" as shown for the bear. Middle contains "row" as shown for the turtle and the ending contains "er" as shown for the club
B. Correct: the image is a bear with a club. The image of the bear and club are most similar. Beginning contains "che" for the bear and the middle contains "ton" as shown for the club
C. Middle contains "ner" as shown for the end of the club
D. Beginning contains "was" as shown for the club and the middle contains "ro" as shown for the turtle

294. D

A. Ending contains "er" as shown for the club

B. Middle contains "row" as shown for the turtle and the ending contains "in" as shown for the bear
C. Middle contains "ton" as shown for the club
D. Correct: The image is of a runner. The image which is most similar is the rabbit since both the runner and rabbit are fast. Ending contains "ila" as shown for the rabbit

295. B

A. Ending contains "ly" as shown for the person throwing something away
B. Correct: The image is of a ships helm. The image of the boat is most similar. Beginning contains "cress" as shown for the boat
C. Beginning contains "cre" as shown for the boat and the ending contains "ly" as shown for the person throwing something away
D. Ending contains "ticent" as shown for the can

296. C

A. Beginning contains "pe" as shown for the can. The middle contains "lo" as shown for the end of the boat and the ending contains "ed" as shown for the money bag
B. Ending contains "lo" as shown for the boat
C. Correct: The image is of a trashcan. The image of the can and of the person throwing away something are most similar. Beginning contains "pe" as shown for the can and the middle contains "at" as shown for the person throwing away something
D. Middle contains "cre" as shown for the beginning of the boat

297. A

A. Correct: The image is of some coins and bills. The image of the money bag is most similar since they are both money related. Beginning contains "ce" as shown for the money bag
B. Ending contains "ent" as shown for the can
C. No words are similar
D. Middle contains "lo" as shown for the end of the ship and the ending contains "bed" as shown for the money bag

298. B

A. Ending contains "ber" as shown for the chess piece

B. Correct: The image is of a baker. The image of the plate is most similar since they are both food related. Ending contains "ay" as shown for the plate

C. Beginning contains "cre" as shown for the sailboat and the ending contains "tay" as shown for the plate

D. Beginning contains "sci" as shown for the plate and the ending contains "ber" as shown for the chess piece

299. D

A. Beginning contains "cre" as shown for the sailboat

B. Ending contains "atay" as shown for the plate

C. Beginning contains "fro" as shown for the chess piece and the ending contains "lo" as shown for the sail boat

D. Correct: The image is a king on their throne. The most similar image is the chess piece as it represents the king in chess. Ending contains "ber" as shown for the chess piece

300. C

A. Ending contains "tay" as shown for the plate

B. Beginning contains "cre" as shown for the sail boat and the middle contains "lit" as shown for the chess piece

C. Correct: The image is a sailor and wheel. The most similar image is the sailboat since the sailor relates to sailing and the tire since it is a wheel. Beginning contains "cre" for the sail boat and the ending contains "ress" as shown for the tire

D. Beginning contains "ress" for the end of the tires and the ending contains "cre" as for the beginning of the sail boat

Made in the USA
Middletown, DE
06 June 2023

32159073R00077